Up the Agency

Up the Agency

Peter Mayle

ST. MARTIN'S PRESS ■ NEW YORK

Design by Judith A. Stagnitto

Library of Congress Cataloging-in-Publication Data

Mayle, Peter.
    Up the agency : the funny business of advertising / Peter Mayle.
       p. cm.
    ISBN 0-312-09930-4
    1. Advertising—United States,   2. Mayle, Peter—Career in
advertising.   I. Title.
HF5813.U6M325 1993
659.1—dc20   93-2561
                                                           CIP

First published in the United Kingdom by Pan Books.
First U.S. Edition: October 1993
10 9 8 7 6 5 4 3 2 1

*To the ladies and gentlemen
of the BBDO London creative
department, 1971–1974*

Thanks for the memories.

Contents

I worked in advertising in New York and London from 1962 until 1975. I started as a junior copywriter and finished as a creative director. I think I was also a vice president, but I never had the cards printed.

It was a good time to be in the business, a period when some brilliant men and women were personally involved in producing advertisements (rather than stroking the barons of Wall Street and the City of London). I was lucky enough to work for three of the best of them.

David Ogilvy taught me to write copy. George Lois taught me about art direction. Bruce Crawford taught me about client handling (an uphill struggle, for him and for me). I am very grateful to them all, and if they had ever been together in one agency, I would probably still be working for them.

I worked for some civilized clients, and I particularly remember the people at Hathaway, Harrods, Olivetti, and Sony for their patience and enthusiasm and their decent manners. They were a pleasure. There were others who weren't—some bullies, some venal clowns, and one or two certifiable paranoiacs—but every industry has runts somewhere in its litter. On the whole, I had a wonderful few years, and it was only when I was promoted well beyond my competence and required to be a businessman that I decided to call it a day.

Since then, advertising has changed. Everybody I spoke to in the course of writing this book has told me so, and it is clear that most of them aren't enjoying the change. Nobody has fun anymore, so they tell me, but the money helps to make it tolerable. Perhaps the business will change again. I hope so, because I remember looking forward to going to work. Despite all the nonsense, I had fun, which to me is as important as money and much more difficult to come by.

I have one apology to make: There is no index. Advertising people usually read advertising books from the back to see whether their names are mentioned in the cast of characters. After taking legal advice, I have mentioned very few names, so I didn't think it necessary to include a Who's Who.

Finally, I would like to thank Frank Lowe for encouraging me to write the book in the first place and for curbing my natural instinct for defamation. To him should go the credit for any restraint you may find in the pages that follow. I'll take the blame for the opinions.

Ménerbes, Provence, France

The codfish lays ten thousand eggs,
The homely hen lays one.
The codfish never cackles
To tell you what she's done.
And so we scorn the codfish,
While the humble hen we prize,
Which only goes to show you
That it pays to advertise.

—Anonymous

I know that half the money I spend on advertising is wasted, and the trouble is I don't know which half.

—Lord Leverhulme

CLIENT: What time is it?
AGENCY: What time would you like it to be?

—attributed to many agencies,
and denied by all

Up the Agency

The Perfect Advertising Man
and His Private Language

Advertising has been variously described as an art, a profession, a sinister instrument of mass persuasion, and a ludicrous waste of money. It hovers on the fringes of big business and show business, of sports and politics, of sleaze and respectability all at once. It is impossible to ignore, and yet most people deny that they are influenced by it. Sometimes it works and sometimes it doesn't. In either case, conclusive proof is hard to come by because of all the other elements involved in persuading millions of people to make a particular choice. It is this—the delightfully imprecise nature of advertising—that makes it such a happy hunting ground for the articulate young person who is convinced he or she has a great idea. Maybe it is indeed a great idea, or maybe it is a piece of twaddle artfully presented, but who's

1

to know? There are no foolproof methods of judging, no truly reliable methods of prediction, no guarantees of success. It's a funny business.

And it attracts some funny people. Most advertising agencies recruit staff on the basis of suspected merit rather than formal qualifications or impressive social backgrounds, and it is a selection process that throws up a rich and varied cast of characters: university graduates, school dropouts, ex-actors, aspiring politicians, assorted corporate misfits, would-be novelists, lay psychologists. There is room for them all, and small fortunes for the lucky ones.

There cannot be many other occupations outside organized crime or entertainment in which money can be made so quickly and at such a young age. Salaries are high and can be doubled within months as a result of a single campaign that is noticed and admired within the business. Agencies have been started from scratch and gone public in the space of five years, making their principals paper millionaires while still in their thirties. And those years spent getting there—the day-to-day working conditions—are by no means brutally arduous or uncomfortable. Offices are well designed and often palatial. Company cars are exotic. Travel is frequent. Eating and drinking in good restaurants is an integral part of the executive's job. Compared to the grind of normal employment, advertising is a most amusing way to spend the working day. Up to a point.

A certain disenchantment sets in, for more people than would publicly admit to it, when the novelty of achievement wears off and they find themselves jumping through the same hoops once too often. In spite of the superficial differences between selling an airline and selling soap, the first requirement of advertising, which is to get somebody to pay for your ideas, doesn't change. The demands imposed on imagination and enthusiasm don't get any less daunting over the years, and meeting those demands becomes increasingly difficult as that first act of persuasion—obtaining approval to spend the money—assumes the familiarity of routine. How many times can you try to convince those skeptical faces across the table that they should buy your campaign? There they sit, responding to what is laid before them with the vivacity of a group of undertaker's mutes while your patience wears thin and you wonder if anything short of dropping your trousers would elicit a reaction. It isn't exciting anymore. It's work.

To some fortunate souls, blessed with the zeal of the true evangelist, this kind of situation is a challenge, even though it has happened hundreds of times before. To others, it finally reaches a stage of such intense tedium that they consider leaving advertising altogether. But for what? Where else would they find the salaries and creature comforts that would be such a wrench to give up? Who will pay for the Mercedes and the lunches? And in any case, what else are they qualified to do? With a handful of exceptions, they stay in the business and console themselves with their standard of living, sometimes cynical, sometimes philosophical, sometimes discontented, but always prosperous.

3

The exceptions are those who have realized that advertising can be a very useful first career. It provides ample opportunity for an intimate study of other people's businesses (whether the clients are bankers or brewers or manufacturers of squeaky toys, they all like their agencies to become "deeply involved"). It provides training in market analysis and the lucid presentation of ideas and recommendations. It offers an interesting course in human nature and the motivations of individuals and large groups alike. It is well paid, and youth is not considered a disadvantage. After ten or fifteen lucrative years, a well-judged leap can take you, still relatively young, into another business where you can start very close to the top.

It happens in politics (at least two current Members of Parliament came from advertising), in the arts (the previous manager of the Metropolitan Opera in New York came from advertising), and in the large financial institutions (Charles Saatchi used to be an advertising writer). The fact that it doesn't happen more frequently is not for lack of opportunity or incentive but because, despite all the grumbling about difficult clients and the high levels of stress and indigestion, advertising is still more diverting than most other legitimate enterprises.

This is largely due to the nature of the advertising beast. There are, God knows, some semicompetent dullards in the business who should have taken up their natural places in the undemanding obscurity of the civil service, but they are comparatively few, because advertising attracts stimulating personalities, not necessarily pleasant or reasonable or trustworthy, but certainly not dull.

If, by some frightful process of genetic packaging, we were able to create the perfect advertising man, what would we find?

Here he is, a shameless extrovert, on a first-name basis with the world. His conversational style is somewhere between the instant familiarity of a TV talk-show host and the soothing bedside manner of a family doctor. He is able to get his foot in the door even over the telephone, never believing no for an answer, temperamentally immune from rebuff, eternally self-confident, rock-solid in his conviction that all manner of good things will come to pass if he can just have half an hour of your time over a drink at the end of the day.

4

He is an immediate enthusiast, capable of developing a passionate interest in the most unlikely subjects as long as they are connected to the product or service that he is working on. A visit to the factory to see how disposable diapers are made? Terrific! A two-day sales conference in Newark? Wonderful! An afternoon with the man who invented perforated tea bags? Fascinating! Deep involvement, the deeper the better, is the breath of life to him.

But should the unthinkable happen and the disposable diaper account go somewhere else, will he brood and despair? Not for long, because he is a man of quite extraordinary resilience. Within days, he will have bounced back. Disposable diapers will have been forgotten in the excitement of a new interest that has plunged him into the absorbing minutiae of double-glazed windows or deodorant socks.

He is not, however, just a receptacle. Once the information has been gathered, it is weighed and processed and arranged so that it provides support for the idea that our man is going to sell to his client. It is here that he will reveal his greatest strength, because he is a superb salesman, leading his audience carefully through a series of reasoned arguments to arrive at an inescapable conclusion. Finally, the idea reflecting this conclusion is unveiled. The campaign is pinned to the wall or shown on the screen while, like a proud father cooing over his firstborn, our man points out the infinite charms on display.

5

There is one last addition to this impressive list of qualities, and it is perseverance. In the long run, this is as important as business acumen or creative ability, and it explains why you will occasionally find agencies that are run by people of outstanding mediocrity. They may not have much in the way of talent, but they have a tenacity of purpose often lacking in their brighter and more flighty colleagues. They stick it out and reach the top, proving that even in advertising there are rewards for solid and unspectacular virtues.

Like most other businesses, advertising has its own collection of labels and euphemisms and pomposities, and as these will appear from time to time in later chapters, it is necessary to explain them.

Most of them spring from a deep-seated desire for commercial respectability, a need to get as far away as possible from the snake-oil salesman and the "Stop me and buy one" era and into the hallowed and profitable ground of professional consultancy. Very large amounts of money are involved here, and all manner of expensive devices and imposing titles have been developed in order to give the simple process of selling a veneer of mystique. No company chairman in his right mind would unquestioningly hand over millions of dollars to a young individual with a bright idea, so the transaction has to be embellished by ritual. In most cases, this is perfectly harmless and makes both parties to the arrangement feel more businesslike. In other cases, it is just deceptive mumbo jumbo, designed to give a raddled sow's ear the appearance of a silk purse. What is confusing to the newcomer, however, is that all agencies, good and bad, are fluent in the kind of terminology that sounds convincingly like value for money.

Here, then, is a discussion of the terms most often used in advertising, starting with the frequently reviled but assiduously courted figure who is central to the whole business.

The Client

Tradesmen have customers, but professional people, from merchant bankers to hairdressers, have clients. In advertising, the client can mean one individual or it can be used in the collective sense to embrace the small herd that will from time to time visit the agency for particularly important meetings. (See Presentations and Pitches, page 12.) Clients are usually less well paid than their agency counterparts, work in less glamorous surroundings, and do not habitually eat in expensive restaurants. This may explain their fondness for the eleven o'clock meeting: a stretched hour and a half of marketing strategy, followed by the startled realization that it's time for lunch, followed inevitably by an invitation from the agency to continue the discussion around the corner at Luigi's.

Commission

The ancestors of today's advertising agents were men who sold space in newspapers. For no extra charge, they would fill the space with a message speaking well of their clients' goods or services. They could afford to do this because they received a sales commission from the newspaper.

In a sense, they still do—not only from the newspapers but from the television and radio stations, the magazine publishers, and the owners of poster sites. There is one price for an advertising agency and a higher one for the individual who buys direct, and the difference is approximately 15 percent. An agency placing a million dollars' worth of ad-

7

vertising should, under these circumstances, receive an income of $150,000.

The commission system has several major faults. When an agency is doing development work on a product that is not being heavily advertised, the commission generated isn't enough to cover the overhead. When the agency is simply placing old work, the commission is often excessive. In neither case is the system equitable.

It also means that agencies have a vested interest (hotly denied, naturally) in recommending ever-larger budgets. Often this is sound commercial advice; sometimes it isn't. But the most obvious absurdity of the system is that it assumes a similar level of competence among all agencies. No distinction is made between the good, the bad, and the indifferent. They all get 15 percent, unless menaced into taking a smaller percentage by a client who makes reduced commission a condition of keeping the business.

There have been sporadic attempts in the past to establish a more rational scale of charges, and some agencies have fee arrangements with some clients, but it would take a concerted effort by the entire industry to change the system. And since it delivers golden eggs to the more fortunate agencies, the goose is likely to remain safe from slaughter.

8

Campaign

A campaign is a collection of advertisements, often spread across TV, press, posters, and radio, that are in theory expressing the same advertising message (the campaign theme) in a variety of ways.

It is also the name of the British industry's organ. *Campaign* magazine, like *Ad Age,* is considered to be essential weekly reading for all advertising people—a position of virtual monopoly that should have encouraged editorial bravery. Instead, the magazine has consistently licked the hand that feeds it, describing nonentities as "supremos" and swallowing inflated agency press releases whole. Visually, it is distinguished by photographs of executives and other notables standing forlornly in what appear to be deserted underground garages.

Copywriters

These are the men and women who write the words, which are sometimes brutally dismissed as "that gray bit under the picture." Good copywriters can transform the fortunes of brands and can earn fortunes doing so. Geoffrey Seymour was the first copywriter in Britain who publicly broke the six-figure barrier, and for a time his name was used in advertising circles as a unit of currency: "A Seymour" was equal to £100,000, "half a Seymour" was £50,000, and so on. The phrase is no longer popular, probably because copywriters earning six-figure salaries are no longer rare.

9

Account Executives

The business given to the agency by the client is known as an account. If it is sufficiently important, it is dealt with by a senior member of the agency, usually on the board, who is called the account director. Beneath the account director are serried ranks of account supervisors, account managers, account executives, and assistant account executives. These poor souls are traditionally the butt of copywriters. One writer, on observing a team of executives filing into a meeting, was overheard describing them as "the bland leading the bland." He was fired, but his epitaph lingers on.

The function of an account executive is to translate the promotional requirements of the client into advertising that will meet those requirements. The best account executives are shrewd business operators and perceptive judges of advertising and human nature. The worst are glorified bag carriers, ferrying messages back and forth between agency and client with all the interpretational skills of a yo-yo.

Art Directors

In more primitive days, people called visualizers were required to devise illustrated settings for the pearls delivered to them from the copywriting department. Simple, paint-stained artisans, they were housed in a remote corner of the agency where clients would never see them. Those days are gone. Visualizers are now called art directors. They often share offices with copywriters (one art director and one copywriter making a "creative team"). They are even introduced to clients when aesthetic matters are being discussed. Their job is to set the visual style of the advertising, from designing the layout to choosing the typeface and selecting an illustrator or photographer. Many modern art directors disdain the traditional skills of doing their own lettering and rough illustration, but to make up for that they have become more involved in the origination of campaign ideas. Or so they like to believe.

Creative Directors

One of the more thankless jobs in an agency is to be responsible for imposing some form of order and discipline on a group of disorderly and undisciplined personalities. Most creative departments have their share of nonconformists and anarchists, and it requires the combined talents of a wet nurse and a prison warden to deal with them. It is no coincidence that various creative directors are prematurely gray.

Producers

When an agency is making a radio or television commercial, the producer is the point of contact between the production company and the rest—writers, art directors, executives, and clients. Producers have two passions: One is working with directors who have made feature films (for the vicarious fame that it brings); the other is going on location (for the out-of-season tan). Producers will always tell you that location jobs are fraught with difficulty, but any suggestion that a Caribbean beach could be faked at Paramount Studios is met with a marked lack of enthusiasm.

Roughs and Storyboards

These are the bare bones of advertising ideas. Roughs are preliminary sketches of posters and press advertisements; storyboards are cartoon-strip versions of proposed TV commercials. The degree of finish depends to a great extent on the degree of understanding and trust that exists between agency and client and on the clarity and strength of the idea. A strong idea can be understood from a scribble on the back of an envelope. A feeble commercial may need a dozen meticulously rendered illustrations to dress up what is essentially a piece of drivel.

Research

The sums of money spent on advertising are such that clients crave reassurance before reaching for their checkbooks. Unwilling or unable to rely on their own and the agency's judgment, they submit their advertising campaigns to members of the public who are selected not because they are knowledgeable about advertising but because they represent the "target audience." It is not uncommon for a campaign to be strangled at birth by a few dozen housewives from Queens. The problem is that any genuinely original idea is likely to receive mixed reviews because of its very originality; show those housewives something familiar and they will give you more comforting reactions. In this way, research often perpetuates tame and derivative work. The results are seen on television every night.

Presentations and Pitches

Very few clients come into an agency and hand over their account without a period of foreplay. The agency's work for other clients may have attracted their attention in the first place, but what they really want to know is, What can you do for *us*?

The only truly candid answer to that question is, *Try it and see*, but as that would sound frivolous and unprofessional, the agency (or, in most cases where a client is on the loose, several competing agencies at the same time) is obliged to put on a show to demonstrate its unique skills. This is the new business presentation.

Its format will differ from agency to agency, but it normally includes the following elements: First comes a private chat with the agency chairman or managing director, during which the agency expresses its deep and sincere interest in the account. After coffee, the client is ushered into the screening room to meet those members of the staff who have been handpicked to work on the account. Their credentials are taken out and polished, and a selection of the agency's work is shown, usually interspersed with remarks on the agency philosophy—that secret weapon that separates a great agency (us) from the also-rans (them). Appetites by now being thoroughly whetted, the meeting adjourns for lunch and further courtship.

This performance may be enough to get the account, or it may lead to a request for more practical evidence of the agency's suitability, a visible answer to the still-unanswered question, What can you do for *us*?

Of all the extravagances in the advertising business, and they are many, nothing is quite so wasteful of time and effort and money as the speculative pitch. It is carrot dangling on the grand scale, employed for the most part by unimaginative clients in the manner of a lame man grasping for a crutch. What happens is that a number of agencies— from two to half a dozen or more, depending on the degree

13

of indecision—will be given a certain amount of information about the account, together with a deadline. Each agency then prepares an advertising campaign, often taking its best people away from their work on existing business and spending thousands of dollars on typesetting, photography, experimental commercials, jingles, new package designs, and anything else that might tip the balance in its favor.

A second round of presentations is arranged for the agencies to show the results of their labors. Eventually, the client can dither no longer. A new agency is appointed, and the losers hurry back to accounts that have been neglected in all the excitement.

The speculative pitch was documented at length some years ago in London's *Sunday Times Magazine* when Guinness moved its £7 million account from one agency to another, only to acquire a campaign of such startling banality that even the winning agency must have been astonished at its luck.

Useful Shorthand

In the daily battle of wits in advertising, where disparate temperaments and sensitivities are thrown together in a highly charged and often panic-stricken atmosphere, there is not always time for the leisurely niceties of corporate behavior. Also, it is not always advisable to say exactly what you think; you may be right or you may be wrong, but a forceful and clear expression of your point of view will probably do more harm than good, since it is certain to cause offense to some of your colleagues or clients. Consequently, a number of euphemisms and shortcuts in communication have been developed over the years; these help to avoid ugly confrontation or the embarrassment of being caught with your trousers down on the wrong side of the fence. A short selection follows:

■ ■ ■

"Basically, the client loves it."—account executive

The client thinks that most of it needs to be done again from scratch, but I can't tell the creative team that. There will be endless argument and I won't be able to get any work out of them for days. If I can find something positive to say, maybe I can nudge the little brutes into some form of cooperation. Anyway, I seem to remember approving it before I took it to the client, so I'd better be careful.

■ ■ ■

"I don't think there'll be a conflict problem. Leave it to me."—agency chairman

If you just stop playing hard to get and give us the business, I'll resign that piddling little account that seems to be worrying you.

■ ■ ■

"Good. We're all agreed, then."—head client

I've decided what I want done. Go away and do it, and stop wasting my time.

■ ■ ■

16

"I've given the package photo a bit of air to make it stand out."—art director

That package is undoubtedly the most badly designed piece of shit I've ever seen, and I've reduced it to the size of a postage stamp so that it doesn't spoil my tasteful layout.

■ ■ ■

"People read books, don't they?"—copywriter

How dare you try to cut my fifteen words of copy down to three sentences! Of course people read long copy. Look at *War and Peace*.

■ ■ ■

"I didn't know the agency had a box at the Met."—client
   Why haven't I been invited?

■ ■ ■

*"Must have lunch as soon as I get back from London/Tokyo/
Bora Bora/Milton Keynes."*—agency managing director
   That should keep you quiet for a couple of weeks,
and with a bit of luck you might have forgotten by the time
I get back.

■ ■ ■

"We'll take care of it on the shoot."—agency TV producer
   If we change the storyboard once more, the director's
going to tell us to stuff it, and he'll go back to L.A.

■ ■ ■

"We tried that, but it didn't work."—creative team
   It's a lousy idea and we have no intention of having
anything to do with it. Why don't you just take what we've
done and sell it?

■ ■ ■

"Creative Boss Quits to Set Up Own Shop."—Ad Age
   He shot his mouth off once too often and now he's
been fired.

17

■ ■ ■

*"As you'll see, there are some very interesting variations in the
responses to the questionnaire."*—research executive
   I'm damned if I know what to make of them, but
maybe one of you can come up with something.

■ ■ ■

"How nice to see you again, sir."—head waiter at the Four
Seasons

It's the third time you've been here this week. God help your liver.

■ ■ ■

"Unfortunately, some of these projections rely rather heavily on the last quarter's performance."—security analyst

Don't try to bullshit me.

■ ■ ■

"The next one's on me."—various

You're paying for lunch.

■ ■ ■

"He's in a presentation."—secretary

I know it's three-thirty, but he's still in the restaurant. Anyway, he doesn't want to talk to you.

■ ■ ■

"I'm sure we'll be able to work out the money angle."—TV production company

Don't be so tight. We all know it's going to cost a fortune.

■ ■ ■

"I'm just sending for a messenger."—studio manager

We'll start on it as soon as we can.

As you can see from some of those coded communications, bad or unpalatable news in advertising is delivered obliquely, and nowhere is this more true than in the situation where, to save large redundancy payments, hints are dropped to an out-of-favor employee that he should look elsewhere.

■ ■ ■

The gentle hint

"You don't mind sharing your secretary for a week or two, do you?"

■ ■ ■

The heavy hint

"The client's having another bad day. I'm coming onto the account for a while to hold his hand."

■ ■ ■

The coup de grace

"We're giving you a new office down the hall by the elevator."

Sorry about that.

The motivations for setting up an agency are *ego* and *money,* probably in that order.

Advertising is a blatantly immodest business, and you will rarely find an agency that follows its own sound advice to clients by adopting a short, descriptive, and memorable name for its product. (There was once an agency called Service Advertising, but it was buried long ago under a pile of forgettable surnames.) Advertising people are addicted to the eponymous, and with very few exceptions their companies are named after themselves, no matter how cumbersome the end result.

The last one to be invited to the christening is, ironically, the person who will have to wrestle with the agency name most often: the long-suffering woman on the switchboard. It is she who has the task of reciting what can sound like the forward line of a multinational soccer team every time the phone rings. Imagine, for example, how you would feel after answering perhaps a hundred calls a day with the seductive greeting "Still Price Twivy Court D'Souza" (believe it or not, a genuine agency name) before you could commence a normal conversation. Two weeks of that is enough to give someone a speech impediment.

One day, agencies may train parrots to take over, but in the meantime what usually happens is that these uncomfortable laundry lists become eroded in use until only the initials or the first couple of names remain. When founding an agency, therefore, it is crucial to get your name at the top end of the list. Failure to do so will lead to relative anonymity, a fate worse than being seen in an unfashionable car.

The only real thing needed to start an agency is a client—preferably a client who spends his money on television rather than in the more labor-intensive and therefore less profitable print media.

With this one potential money-maker as collateral, the members of the new agency can make their first clandestine presentation. Taking an afternoon off from work—they will still be holding on to their old jobs, just in case—they will submit their plans for a golden future to a bank. They need money for premises, for cars and lunches (because appearances will have to be kept up), and for salaries. They will not normally receive any income from their client until the advertising has actually appeared. Before that can happen, the work has to be produced and paid for and the TV time and press space has to be bought. The members of the media like to be paid within thirty days; clients often take up to ninety days to pay the agency. The unpleasantly long gap

21

between forking it over and raking it in, with interest accumulating at the rate of several zeros a day, is one of the hazards of launching a new agency.

That, however, is a problem that can at least be foreseen and measured. The real hazard, more fundamental and infinitely less predictable, is how the new agency's founders are going to work together. It is one thing to be united in a common disdain for your tyrannical and money-grubbing employers, who wouldn't recognize a good advertisement if it got into bed with them. It is quite another thing to find yourself and your new colleagues in the position of having nobody to complain about except one another. Getting on with one partner whom you can tolerate over a period of years without wanting to throttle is hard enough, but getting on with three or four partners is almost miraculous, and such miracles are few and far between. The corporate divorce rate in advertising is high, and the pages of the trade press are spattered with breathless pieces of prose reporting breakaways, boardroom rifts, and filched accounts, complete with sour quotes from those who consider themselves wronged and want to put in their two cents (*no comment* being the words most ardently hoped for but most seldom used).

But those days of high drama are still ahead. For the moment, the new agency's founders are busy presenting a united and enthusiastic front to anyone who will listen to them.

Traditionally, agencies are started by individuals who can bring different but complementary skills to the partnership. The old favorite—three young people walking around in alphabetical order—consists of an account executive, a copywriter, and an art director. These three, if they are sufficiently well known in the industry, will enjoy a period of limelight and novelty, maybe lasting for months, when they will give interviews to the business press and presentations to prospective clients. A "prospective client," in this atmosphere of overcranked optimism, is someone from a client organization who can be persuaded to accept lunch from you; a "hot prospect" is someone who can be persuaded to visit the agency without the benefit of lunch.

The gist of the interviews and presentations is the same: the reason, other than ego and money, why yet another agency should be added to the 640 agencies that already exist. The difficulty here is that there is only one valid commercial reason for a client to change agencies, and that is to get more effective advertising. It won't be significantly cheaper or produced any more quickly. The meetings won't necessarily be any more stimulating. The working lunches will be just as earnest. All the client can hope for at the end of the day is that the work produced by the eager trio will be better than his existing advertising; and that, as any realist will admit, is not a result that can be guaranteed. So it comes down to a question of confidence. If the prospective client can be made to feel that there is a justifiable chance of getting better value for his advertising money, he might take it.

The bait offered by new agencies to inspire confidence will vary in the way it is stuck on the hook, but it will usually be a combination of three elements, with the emphasis changing according to the personalities and abilities involved.

First, credentials have to be established. As the agency is new, it won't have a track record of successful case histories with which to dazzle the audience. So, necessity being the mother of appropriation, it borrows them. The founders pool their past efforts, taking care to forget the flops, and wheel out an array of household names and famous cam-

2 3

paigns on which they have worked. The connections in some cases are best described as tenuous. It is not unknown for two or three copywriters with conveniently faulty memories to give the modest but definite impression that each of them was responsible for the same campaign. Since any long-running campaign will have received contributions from a number of writers, this kind of creative slipstreaming is almost impossible to disprove. So it is with executives who have been "associated" with a successful brand. The implication is that they steered it to success; the reality is often different but, unfortunately, less impressive.

Thus in one way or another, with or without scruples, the new agency is able to equip itself from the start with a convincing and familiar body of work.

The second element in the presentation is where bullshit meets science. Advertising people are trained to ferret out minor differences among competing but similar products and to promote what they feel will be the difference that makes the sale. With commendable faith, they will often apply this technique to themselves, imposing severe strains on credibility and syntax alike. Their intention is to distill their own methods of working into an easily digested formula—their very own agency philosophy—and give it a label that separates it from all the other formulas being bandied around by their competitors. A great deal of time and ingenuity is devoted in these early and desperate days to getting it right. Or if not right, at least different.

One of the most energetically trumpeted agency philosophies was devised many years ago by Ted Bates, the American agency. It was based on the premise that every product could be given a "unique selling proposition" (but only by Ted Bates, who had the secret). This phrase has now passed into general advertising language, possibly because it

2 4

is two-thirds perfect: *Unique* and *selling* are words that can, and indeed did, evoke an almost Pavlovian response among clients. And there have been other magical recipes, equally sharply defined, if not so seductively worded: the prime prospect, the four-point process, the reduction of risk through research, the pre-emptive factor, the dormant benefit—dozens of them, all attempting to reduce the complex and uncertain process of persuasion down to a simple certainty. Alas, for agencies and clients, certainties don't exist. As long as there is room for free and intelligent choice in society, they never will exist, and no amount of behind-the-scenes waffle can do more than provide a rational introduction to what may look like an irrational idea. Agency philosophies are, at best, common sense dressed up as the Holy Grail and, at worst, specious and cynical bunk.

The final element in a new agency's presentation can be, for a limited time, very attractive. It goes something like this:

> Here we are, experienced, talented, and hungry. We have left our comfortable jobs with big agencies because we had to spend more time administering and delegating than preparing advertisements. We have seen what happens in big agencies when the honeymoon period is over, when clients used to dealing with the managing director are palmed off with beardless boys, when the best brains of the agency are busy on someone else's account. But if you give your business to us, we personally will devote our enormous energies and skills to it. We, the proprietors, will cherish your business as though it was our own (which, of course, it is). You will *always* be able to pick up the phone and talk to the boss.

This is all very well and even true, up to a point. But the question sitting up and begging at the end of the conference table is what will happen to the delightful intimacy of the proposed arrangement if the new agency should get another account, or another dozen accounts. The question is rarely pursued, because any remotely perceptive client knows the answer. He will just have to hope that the founders of the agency are confident enough of their own talents to hire equally talented people as their business grows. In the meantime, the client will benefit from the fact that new agencies need to make their mark with their first accounts, and he is likely to get the best that they can give in the way of service and creativity.

If their best is good enough, it won't be long before the agency starts to make its presence felt. The advertising community spends a lot of time in bars and restaurants gossiping about itself. One good opening campaign and some adroit self-promotion can have an effect out of all proportion to the agency's size and accomplishments. It becomes *hot*.

Stocking the Zoo, and the
Joys of Management

One of the more solemn clichés in advertising is that the real assets of an agency are the people who work in it. And it's true: The ability to attract and keep talented staff is generally considered to be almost as important as bringing in new clients. In many ways, however, it is more difficult. Clients tend to be rational. They are used to working within certain corporate disciplines. They look for steady progress in their careers, and they are prepared to exercise patience as they climb toward the giddy eminence of a seat on the board. You can reason with clients—most of them, anyway.

Advertising people, in contrast, tend to be impatient, often irrational, usually impulsive, and almost always egotistical. These qualities, while useful and necessary in dictators, produce troublesome employees, and for the management of an advertising agency, maintaining some kind of productive harmony among the rank and file is like getting the Italian army to march in step. Not only do they have to contend with the outbreaks of greed, ambition, and office feuds that occur in any business but there is also a fundamentally disruptive element peculiar to advertising that is guaranteed, sooner or later, to cause grief and conflict. It is the creative department.

Creative people are not temperamentally suited to the orderly routine of office life. They find conventional working hours inconvenient. Meetings bore them. Clients exasperate them. Deadlines are beneath their consideration. They will spend weeks apparently doing nothing about a crucial job despite entreaties and threats, and then, just before the ax comes down on their necks, they will work all weekend and expect applause and sympathy on Monday morning. They are intransigent and highly opinionated, and yet often curiously inarticulate when it comes to justifying those opinions. They take criticism badly and sulk easily. They are constantly demanding more money than there is in the budget, bigger spaces and longer time periods than there are in the media plan, and extensions to the deadlines they accepted or ignored weeks ago. Because of their occasional triumphs and because, in the end, nobody else in the agency can do what they can do, they get away with behavior that should have gotten them thrown out on the street.

All this, of course, is about as popular as halitosis with their colleagues, particularly account executives, who have egos of their own and who see themselves as being equally necessary to the agency's daily business. Account executives want to keep their clients happy. Creative people want to do work that will make them famous. In theory, these two aims are not mutually exclusive, but in practice very few campaigns are ever produced without friction and disagreement, and occasionally the odd drops of blood are visible on the office carpet.

It's entirely predictable. The creative people have spent their customary weeks walking around the problem, sharpening their pencils, playing darts, and generally getting themselves prepared for a visit from their muse. The account executives watch the days go by and fend off increasingly insistent demands from the client, who is anxious to see what next year's millions are going to be spent on. Finally, the campaign is presented within the agency and someone has the temerity to suggest that changes are necessary (as they usually are).

Stunned disbelief from the writer and art director ensues. They retire hurt to a convenient restaurant, tossing their curls and muttering darkly about stupidity and compromise. The account executives commiserate with one another about having to deal with overpaid children. When work resumes, as it must, because by now the client is sputtering with impatience, there is a distinct absence of friendly and respectful collaboration. It is advertising's version of the eternal conflict between art and commerce, and the only people in the agency who can observe it with the detached amusement it deserves are the mail-room boy and the cleaning lady.

Everyone else is affected. From the secretary who is on the receiving end of a copywriter's sulk to the financial director who queries a bundle of wine-stained and incomprehensible expenses from an art director, nobody is completely immune from the mysterious ways in which creative people move and the interminable sparring that goes on between them and the rest of the world. But that's the

2 9

nature of the business, and the compensations for putting up with a little strife each day are considerable.

There are four, or in exceptional circumstances five, varieties of inducement used by agency managements to hang on to their employees. Although they are set out here as a series of steps up a single ladder, it is very unlikely that one individual will stay long enough to complete the course with one agency, because changing agencies is a quicker way to make the quantum leap from getting a salary to getting a slice of the action. But, if you should stay put, your brilliant career in advertising will proceed as follows.

Money

To start with, there will only be money. It will probably be more than you could earn in most other businesses (apart from the freak money being picked up by adolescent bond traders on Wall Street), but that's all it will be—a paycheck, subject to tax and, even worse, with no visible status attached to it. However, if you have any kind of aptitude and a reasonably intelligent and perceptive boss, it won't be long before the thought of losing you to another agency will provoke the generous reflex that moves you up a step.

3 0

More Money, and a Company Car

It won't, at this stage, be one of the black Porsches so dear to the hearts of middle-aged advertising executives (which is why they're known as MenoPorsches), or even the beginner's BMW that sits, with dozens like it, in city garages. But it's a start, and if you shop around, you might be able to swing something a little out of the ordinary, such as a Harley-Davidson or a VW convertible. The great thing is to get a car that couldn't possibly belong to a Procter & Gamble sales rep.

A Title

Your next step takes you out of the purely material rewards and into the officially anointed hierarchy. There are almost as many artfully contrived titles in advertising as there are in the Debrett's—meaningless to the outside world, perhaps, but of enormous significance to the recipient. (Where else but in advertising would you find a man desperate enough to have International Deputy Vice Chairman printed on his business cards?) Your title will depend on your field of expertise, but it will usually include one or more of the following: supervisor, group head, Executive (with a capital *E*), senior personal (as in personal assistant), joint or co- (as in cocreative director), and so on. Nuance is all-important, and those who invent and bestow titles have to be very careful that by pleasing you they don't deliver a terminal blow to the self-esteem of some of your colleagues. Anyway, that's their problem. You have your title and, naturally, more money and a better car.

3 1

A Share in the Equity

Now we come to the main move. This could set you up for life—or, if not life, at least for the next five years— and it causes untold agonizing in agency boardrooms. If you have become invaluable—by consistently producing good campaigns, let's say, or by ingratiating yourself so thoroughly with a big client that he will follow you wherever you may wander—the top management of your agency will be obliged to nail you to the desk. This is a disagreeable situation for them, because it means that they will have to dig not only into their wallets but into their closely guarded hoard of shares in the agency, and there will always be one or two shareholders who will dispute the need to reduce their personal holdings in order to humor a young kid like you. Hence the agonizing. But what else can be done? They've tried keeping you quiet with a Ferarri, with a higher salary, fatter expenses, and the most important title they can think of, but they have nightmares that you and a significant slice of business will go and do something silly like start another agency. There's nothing for it but to give you a share of the equity and a nice restrictive contract. This is done with varying degrees of good grace and everyone gets back to work.

Your Name on the Door

That is as far as it goes for the majority of people who make successful careers in advertising, and it's enough, if the agency prospers and goes public, to make them millionaires. But what is mere money to someone who has been trying to keep the lid on a rabid ego all these years? There is a high incidence of egomaniacs in advertising, and they will not be satisfied until they have achieved the fifth and ultimate level of success; they have to be *seen* to own part of the agency. They want their name everywhere: on the door, on the letterhead, on the envelopes, on the compliments slips and the receptionist's lips, and—the big thrill—on the stock-market listing. If they are sufficiently determined and sufficiently important to the future prosperity of their partners, they will get their way, requiring another heavy bill for reprinted stationery, another eulogy disguised as a press release, another placated ego.

And yet, looked at when the first warm glow of self-satisfaction has faded, there is still something . . . not quite right. The name will be visible, certainly, but it will be the last horse in the race. The agency name may have become Still Price Twivy Court D'Souza *and Jenkins,* but we all know what happens to those names that dangle at the end of a long list. They drop off. In practical terms of everyday usage, they might as well not be there. If one looks at it cynically (and cynicism does, from time to time, creep into these matters), adding to the agency's name to keep a valued colleague from arranging a mutiny costs little and means less.

Ability is quickly rewarded in advertising, and the whole process that has just been described can be completed within ten years. If you make a couple of well-considered jumps from one agency to another, it might not even take that long, and therein lies the second ever-present problem for management, just as tiresome and occasionally more damaging than the war of attrition with the creative department. Rumor stalks the halls of every advertising agency, encouraging ambition and impatience with stories of salaries being doubled, five-figure bonuses, turbo-charged Maseratis, and all those other plums that are falling into the laps of anyone who is good enough to play the game of agency leapfrog. It is most unsettling. Why, any day now another agency that has just pulled a fat account could call you up and make you an offer you can't believe, and if you've been having a normal abrasive time with the idiots that you work with, you will be hard put to turn it down. (The thought of encountering more, and maybe worse, idiots in the other agency doesn't occur to you yet.)

Your management will know all about this kind of inducement because they do it themselves when they want to hire someone of established ability. They are also aware that some agencies, either because they're stuffed with cash or hiring specifically for a major account, will make offers that simply can't be matched in material terms. But even in advertising, money isn't everything, and a handful of the better-run agencies are able to keep their best people without beating them about the ears every three months with a checkbook.

They do it by providing what corporate psychologists would call job satisfaction, one of those wonderfully vague but all-embracing phrases that can mean all things to all people and that looks so neat and tidy on personnel reports. In fact, it is neither neat nor easy to define, since it is made up of so many intangibles, but there are certain characteristics common to those few agencies that enjoy a high degree of staff loyalty and a correspondingly low rate of staff turnover.

The first and perhaps the most important of these is the reputation within the business. When an agency's work is widely admired, when it picks up awards, and always providing it isn't run by a bunch of Nazis, it becomes thought of as a desirable place to work. If you already work there, you are automatically part of an elite, and few things are more comforting to the human soul than a feeling of superiority.

Another essential is to keep everyone so busy that they haven't got time to be bored. Boredom leads to all kinds of mischief—politics and vendettas, moonlighting, four-hour lunches, disastrous liaisons with secretaries, and all the rest of it. Agencies need to be kept slightly understaffed and slightly overworked, and an occasional bout of disciplined panic and "ghosting" (working through the night) is no bad thing.

But this will only be effective as long as the advertising produced within the agency consistently sees the light of day. When campaigns are mauled or rejected by clients after a lot of effort and overtime have been expended, it is difficult to persuade copywriters and art directors (who bruise easily) that they should try again. It's no fun for the account executive. It costs the agency twice as much as it should to produce an acceptable piece of work. But above all, it is a dispiriting blow to morale, and if it happens too often, it is only a matter of time before word gets around and the best people get out. Successful and highly regarded agencies always have at least one person at the top who is capable of selling 80 percent of the advertising he or she takes to the client. Providing this can be kept up, such persons are worth their weight in expenses.

The other aspects of agency management, apart from the obvious requirement to keep generating new business, are details. They may be as important as using income and profits intelligently, or as trifling as organizing a good office party, but they are all secondary to the way the human assets are managed. Agencies don't become rich and famous because of their impeccable administrative procedures or even their financial acumen, but because one or two people at the top have been able to hold together a collection of wildly conflicting personalities and motivate them into working with one another. It is not a skill that can be learned mechanically; it is a knack, rather like being good with animals.

35

36

Every agency has to live with the awful possibility that, for one reason or another, a large client will leave, causing headlines and redundancies and, worst of all, public doubts about the agency's stability and prospects of survival. Is it going through one of those periods of internecine warfare known as a management shake-up? Is there a plot afoot to start a breakaway agency? Does the departing client know something we don't know? These and other fascinating and damaging speculations are energetically promoted by those with axes to grind and advantage to be gained. Hearsay and wishful thinking are retailed as fact, and sometimes they will have the desired effect: The agency's remaining clients will become unsettled. Indeed, some of them may be so sensitive about being associated with what they are repeatedly told is a sinking ship that they will scuttle off in the appropriate fashion.

The only way to avoid this nightmare is to ensure that new clients come in faster than old ones leave. Any losses can then be airily dismissed as unfortunate casualties of the agency's dynamic expansion. Consequently, all agencies have a more or less organized program designed to pull in new accounts. (At one time, this was called soliciting new business, which was thought to have a respectable ring about it until it was pointed out that the only other trade commonly known to solicit for a living was prostitution, and so alternative terminology had to be found.)

Some of the larger agencies maintain a small squad of corporate poachers whose sole job it is to cultivate contacts and tickle them into a sufficiently receptive mood for a presentation. In other agencies, the principals have to assume these duties in addition to working for the clients they already have, and this is their excuse for the out-of-office diversions we shall come to later.

In the new business budget, a certain amount will be put aside for speculative pitches, which can cost anything from a few thousand dollars for rough layouts to $100,000 or more for a full-blown campaign with commercials. There will also be provision for the occasional advertisement (but only occasional; agencies tend not to spend too much on advertising) placed in the business press to commemorate some particularly impressive achievement, such as a clutch of new accounts or a demonstrably effective campaign. And there will be the mailing shots, aimed at everyone within postal range who might conceivably be influenced by developments within the agency: a new appointment to the board, an addition to the range of services on offer, an award here, a research breakthrough there, the acquisition of another agency—triumph piling upon triumph to foster the image of growth and success.

But of all the techniques used to convert someone else's client into your own, perhaps none is so enthusiastically employed as that mysterious and fattening process that appears with such regularity on expense accounts and that is optimistically described as "entertaining a prospective client." This covers practically every social and sporting activity known to man, and much else besides, but it starts with simple refreshment.

Nothing of any significance in the advertising business is discussed without a glass or a knife and fork close at hand, and it was probably an advertising man who was guilty of inventing the hideously uncivilized custom of the *business breakfast*. That, however, is not generally forced upon clients until they are safely in the bag. In any case, breakfast does not allow enough time for the delicate probing and maneuvering that is the purpose of the first rendezvous. Dinner, at this early stage of the relationship, is too intimate. But lunch is perfect.

The choice of restaurant requires very careful thought, not because of an interest in good food, which is of little or no importance on these occasions, but because of psychological and practical factors. First, does the restaurant reflect the way in which the agency would like to be regarded? The image of a young and irreverent agency doesn't sit comfortably with ties and solemn conversation at the Plaza, any more than a pinstriped executive from a conservative agency would feel at home in one of those frisky Italian establishments where the waiters are prone to kiss you on both cheeks and pinch your bottom. And then there are the prospective client's feelings to be considered. One wants him to be relaxed and comfortable and, at the same time, stimulated by his surroundings (which include you) so that he can appreciate how dull his existing agency is. It's a question of matching what little you so far know of your guest's personality with any one of dozens of possibilities. When in doubt, the instinct is to take the most expensive option rather than risk leaving the prospective client with the feeling that he has been underlunched.

To add to the complications, the choice is limited to restaurants where the host has clout. To be treated as just another customer and consigned to a murky little table by the kitchen is an appalling blow to the image and could ruin the mood of the entire lunch. The agency executive must be seen to be in control—with a good but discreet table and no small measure of deference from the staff. Obviously, this can be guaranteed only by frequent visits and consistent overtipping, and so time and money need to be invested in becoming a familiar and well-loved figure in maybe half a dozen restaurants. To the uninformed observer, the sight of an advertising executive having lunch with his secretary might indicate a liaison that goes beyond work. In fact, he is merely doing his duty, preparing the ground and building up credit in the restaurant against the day when he will bring the prospective client to the table.

And when he does, to the accompaniment of bowing and scraping and solicitous inquiries after his health and confidential disclosures about a speciality that is not on the menu but is available to privileged clients, then he is able to concentrate on his poacher's work, secure in the knowledge that he is *in charge*. Settling back amid a flurry of waiters, he can devote himself to stage one: purposeful small talk.

Nothing as crass as the true purpose of lunch will be mentioned during the first two courses. Instead, like a doctor examining a new patient to see if he can find any interesting deformities, the agency executive will gently interrogate his guest to determine his areas of general interest. Does he like tennis, golf, sailing, the opera, nightclubs? Where does he spend his vacations? Does he watch films, read books, go to art exhibitions? What are his politics? Little by little, it comes out and is stored for future reference while the agency executive waits for the right moment to broach, with infinite tact and finesse, the two most important questions of all.

First, is the client secure in his job and in control of his business? If he isn't, and is honest enough to admit it, he might find that lunch ends early; it is, after all, his account we're after, not his conversation, and if there are doubts about his ability to deliver, he is not a man to waste time cultivating. There are many ways to clarify this fundamental point, the most flattering of which is also the most risky. It is to ask the client whether he had ever thought of putting his immense skills at the disposal of an agency, where men of his caliber are always in demand. This sometimes backfires. Instead of the client being highly complimented but not interested, he may very easily jump at the hint and start asking awkward questions about company cars and a seat on the board.

But let's assume that he is a serious prospect, dedicated to his brand and with the power to move the account. Once this has been established, the agency executive can move on to the second crucial point: How strong are the client's ties with his existing agency? The fact that he is breaking bread with a competitor is not necessarily significant. Some clients see it as part of their job to keep in touch with a number of agencies on an informal basis. Others are just gluttons with a fondness for free lunches (they can usually be spotted by their choice of food and drink, and by

40

the glazed and unseeing eye that ignores the arrival of the bill).

The time to bring up the subject of the client's relationship with his agency is traditionally at the end of the meal, over coffee. Why this should be, when both parties know perfectly well why they are sitting down together, is somewhat of a mystery, but it is a carefully observed part of the ritual. If things have gone particularly well and a rapport is in the making, brandy and cigars may be summoned as a means of prolonging the conversation, and then the agency executive will roll up his sleeves and start chipping away.

This is an exercise in heroic restraint, wonderful to watch. The agency executive may feel that the client's current advertising stinks. He may know, because he is an avid gatherer of gossip, that the people who produce it loathe one another and drink too much, or that they subcontract the work out to free-lance moonlighters. None of this will be mentioned—not in so many words, anyway. The agency executive will be quite happy to sow a seed or two of doubt while appearing to be scrupulously fair. He may even be generous with faint praise, because the true purpose of lunch is not to make an unseemly grab at the business there and then. It is to offer himself—wise, sympathetic, and *highly professional*—as a potential port in an advertising storm if anything should cast a blight on the client's existing arrangements. If he has achieved this, and if in addition he has picked up some valuable information about his guest's leisure interests, then the lunch can be counted as worthwhile.

Depending on the time of the year and the proclivities of the client, lunch will be followed by an invitation to the U.S. Open, a concert at the Met, a day of golf, a private screening of a feature film, or some other appropriate event. Many of these invitations will include the client's wife, so

41

that there can be no doubt that this is a purely social occasion. Other members of the agency will be present, of course, but not in any official capacity, and there will be no mention of business; this is merely a group of congenial people enjoying themselves.

Weeks or months, sometimes years, will go by, but contact will be maintained and the invitations will continue in the hope that patience will be rewarded. Often, it is. Sooner or later, the client will have some reason to be discontented with his existing agency. It might be the departure of a key executive, disagreements about a new campaign, or simply a gradual realization that the magic has gone out of the marriage. For whatever reason, the client feels that it's time for someone to take a fresh and enthusiastic look at his advertising problems. And whom does he turn to? Who else but those congenial people with whom he has already spent so many happy hours.

Agencies may dispute the importance of entertaining, because it smacks of buying business rather than winning it on merit. (And, in fairness, most accounts are won through abilities other than proficiency at lunch.) Nevertheless, it is not uncommon for a diligent seeker after new business to eat and drink his way through several hundred dollars a week, and there are one or two legends in their own lunchtime whose only notable business assets are their extraordinary social stamina, their seemingly indestructible livers, and their thick skins. These men follow the advertising version of the philanderer's golden rule: If you ask a hundred women to go to bed with you, ten of them probably will.

Eating and drinking as part of the job is not confined to the senior members of agencies. Everybody does it, in surroundings of diminishing luxury and elegance according to rank and salary, and there is at every level a clear under-

42

standing of who picks up the bill. Account executives buy lunch for copywriters as an inducement to further creative effort. Copywriters buy lunch for art directors, who claim they never have any money. Television production companies buy lunch for agency producers. Media sellers buy lunch for agency media buyers, and so it goes. There are probably a hundred restaurants in New York whose prosperity is due almost entirely to the appetites and thirst of the advertising business, and if there was ever to be a single slogan representative of the industry, it would surely be those three irresistible words: *"Let's have lunch."*

Great Moments in
the Working Day

The official agency day begins at 9:00 A.M. and ends at 5:30 or 6:00 P.M., but only novices and conscientious receptionists pay much attention to the formal hours of business. The ambitious members of the agency—or rather, those who don't mind their ambition showing—will be at their desks long before nine, knowing that the early morning is the best time to get some constructive memo writing done before they are sucked into the vortex of briefings, presentations, lunches, and drinks that will take up the rest of the day.

There is, however, one oasis of calm: the creative department is often tranquil and virtually deserted until 9:30 or even later, since copywriters and art directors like to exercise their artistic privilege to ignore such prosaic habits as punctuality. The creative director, now retired, of a large agency once became so irritated at being the only member of his department to start work on time that he lay in wait at the entrance to the agency, alarm clock in hand, to hurl abuse and threats at latecomers. As ten o'clock approached, he was about to return to his office, when a final languid art director sauntered through the door.

"You should have been here an hour ago," said the creative director.

"Why?" said the artist. "What happened?"

But eventually, with bright or bleary eyes, the entire agency is present and ready to attack the problems (which, as all advertising people know, are only opportunities in disguise) of the day. These are dealt with in a variety of ways that tend to overlap, but they are probably best explained as separate events. And to start with, what better than the corporate ritual dance without which nothing from the purchase of office china to the takeover of a rival agency can proceed: the inescapable, interminable meeting.

The prize for the most trivial meeting is currently held by a team of thirteen agency and television production people who agonized over which brand of mineral water should be available on the set where they were shooting. (Badoit won, but not without some stiff competition from the Perrier supporters.)

Whatever is on the agenda, though, is subject to the same rules and traditions that govern the conduct of all meetings and the deportment of those in attendance.

Venue

Unless the numbers are exceptionally large, or the subject particularly important, meetings are held in the office of the most senior person involved. At the moment when the meeting is scheduled to start, the senior person will usually contrive to be on the phone so that less exalted colleagues can be instructed by the secretary to wait outside or to tiptoe in and perch awkwardly on the glove-leather furniture until the telephone is put down. It is instantly picked up again, and the secretary is buzzed and told to hold all further calls. The senior person, sighing at the magnitude of the cares of high office, will then be ready to preside.

A variation on the telephone technique used to be practiced by the senior vice president of a large New York agency. As his underlings filed in, he would peel off a twenty-dollar bill from a fist-sized roll of bills and use it to polish his already gleaming toe caps before crumpling it up and throwing it into the waste basket. The effect diminished with repetition, but young and impressionable executives could often be seen in their cubbyholes imitating the great man, the only difference being that memos were used on the toe caps instead of currency.

Equally effective as an unusual start to a meeting, and much closer to nature, was the habit of an agency chairman to be closeted in his personal executive bathroom as the appointed hour arrived. And so one would wait in his office, eye and ear irresistibly drawn to the closed door in the corner, until, with a triumphant flush and a gurgle from the sink, the door would open and the chairman would emerge to address himself to more intellectual matters.

These and other refinements are only possible when meetings are held in a private office, where twenty-dollar bills can be rescued discreetly from the wastebasket and where lavatories are only a few steps from the desk. Other tactics need to be used when the meeting is of sufficient size and gravity to justify the more formal setting of the agency conference room. In this case, the senior person should always be the last to arrive, preferably still in conversation on a cordless phone or with a secretary in tow taking dictation on foot.

Details such as these, while they may be considered bizarre or bad-mannered, are necessary in order to make it clear who is in charge. "Every cock," as the old proverb reminds us, "is king of his own dunghill."

Pecking Order and Deportment

Junior people arrive first, if they know what's good for them, followed in ascending order of seniority by the others. Layouts, computer printouts, and files should be carried loose—never in an attaché case, which arouses suspicions that you were late getting into the office and haven't had time to extract the relevant documents. As the papers are shuffled and coffee is sipped, the nominal leader of the meeting (as opposed to the true leader, who is the senior person) will make an opening statement about the decision that confronts the assembled gathering. It may be to set a level of advertising expenditure, to assess a new campaign, to ponder the merits of a brilliant but promotion-hungry executive, to interpret a turgid piece of research, or to work out how best to deal with a client who has expressed a willingness to accept free airline tickets. The subject having been put "on the table," the meeting turns its attention to the most junior member present, who is expected to give an opinion.

A nasty moment indeed, particularly if minutes are being taken that will subsequently be circulated and that might easily be used in evidence at some embarrassing future

47

date. A slip of the tongue here could jeopardize chances of promotion, that new BMW, and upgrading to business-class on business trips. Why in God's name do they have to put the least experienced person on the spot first?

One might think that it is the proper beginning for a truly democratic decision-making process in which every voice, however small and unimportant, has its say. It is nothing of the sort. The reason for soliciting opinions from the bottom upward is to ensure that the senior person, whose judgment is obviously delivered last, doesn't make a fool of himself by overlooking an obvious point that could render his wisdom suspect. He, after all, doesn't have the time to pore over the fine print of every piece of paper that comes across his desk; that is minions' work. The senior person is there to assess the information presented to him and then to decide on a course of action that will steer the agency ever onward and upward.

So the junior member says his piece and the others try to gauge how it has been received before it's their turn. If there is an encouraging nod from the senior person, the next in line to speak will elaborate on what has just been said, adding a few flourishes or, to be on the safe side, a couple of minor concerns. This continues up the pecking order until it is clear that a consensus is there for the reaching. The senior person seizes it, adding a flourish or two of his own, and everyone gets back to work. It has been a *good meeting*.

But, given the assortment of egos and ambitions that exist in any agency, good and constructive meetings do not happen all that often, and it is much more likely that there will be a healthy measure of conflict. Advertising is a matter of opinion rather than a matter of fact, and there is little in the way of indisputable proof that can be used to demolish the misguided ideas of the lunatic who opposes you. This leads, at best, to reasoned argument followed by deadlock; at worst, to veiled insults, sulking, studied inattention to the other point of view, passing notes to a supporter, gusty sighs of boredom, and other, less wholesome signals of disagreement—nail clipping, nose picking, muffled belches, investigation of the inner ear with the end of a pencil, or any minor distraction that can be achieved short of physical violence.

This puts the senior person in a quandary because the meeting is not getting anywhere, and a choice has to be made between democracy and dictatorship. Democracy is tiresome and time-wasting, but at least it keeps most people more or less happy, whereas dictatorship can lead to mutiny in the ranks, resignations, and potential problems with the client. Not surprisingly, democracy usually wins—"we all need to give this a little more thought"—and another date is fixed so that everyone can lock horns again next week. With a little luck, some vigorous lobbying during the intervening days can modify attitudes and prepare the ground for a good meeting—the result, naturally, of mature reassessment. Compromise is never mentioned. Compromise is for wimps.

The Act of Creation

Eventually, some of the decisions made at meetings have to be given form and substance and turned into advertising, and for sheer drama, unconscious comedy, and excitement, nothing can approach the speculative new business pitch.

The agency is given a brief and a deadline by the client (who has decided after some exploratory discussions to give these bright people a chance). A creative team is allocated to the task, a date is set to review their endeavors, and everyone involved waits, with varying degrees of impatience and optimism, for the act of creation to take place. The time allowed for this can be as little as a few days or as much as several weeks, but somehow it is never enough; creative people are instinctive procrastinators, and they consider it unwise to complete work in advance of a deadline, because this might encourage their colleagues to try to change what they've done. Experienced executives realize this and will often set a fake deadline. Experienced creative people will assume that it's fake and disregard it. But that is only one aspect of the complicated and often puzzling process by which a bundle of documents becomes a campaign.

Whatever the product or service being advertised, there are certain standard but unhelpful vague criteria that all good agencies insist upon. (Bad agencies have only one criterion: Give the client what he wants.)

The first requirement is that the advertising should be intrusive. It will be competing for attention with editorial matter, with TV and radio shows, with films, or, in the case of posters, with traffic. If the message isn't noticed, it's money down the drain.

There is a school of thought that claims producing noticeable advertising is relatively simple; just get a woman to take her clothes off and feign some sympathy with the product. A carefully structured piece of research will confirm that this does indeed attract attention from both men and women. However, if you're advertising frozen peas or tennis rackets, the uncontrived and persuasive connection between naked flesh and the product is not immediately obvious. So being noticeable isn't enough; the advertising should be relevant, as well.

It should also be distinctive within its own category

so that it stands out from competing brands and services. It should also be persuasive. It should also be memorable. It should also be on the creative director's desk by the end of next week. Small wonder that the members of our creative team, electrified by the challenge and opportunity for greatness that confronts them, feel the need for a long and reflective lunch.

In addition to the technical details under discussion—the length of the TV spots, the size of the press ads, the inadequacy of the brief, and the lack of time—there are two more personal considerations to be taken into account. The first is mentioned quite openly, and it is the mutual desire of writer and art director to produce a campaign of such brilliant originality that the entire industry will notice it, talk about it, and bestow upon it the supreme accolade of a *major award*. (As we shall see later, there are a number of these given out every year, and since they are instrumental in procuring job offers, promotion, salary increases, and a moment of fame, they are deeply loved.)

The second, even more personal hope, is not talked about. Although in theory the creative team should march hand in hand as they proceed toward the great idea, in practice each of them wants to get there first, to be the originating genius: I did it; he helped. This arouses the critical faculties, as far as the other person's suggestions are concerned, to a degree that can cause days of stalemate and a feeling of tension in the creative team's office, which any seasoned executive learns to expect. In fact, it adds to the reputation for being difficult that creative people secretly enjoy. Artists are always difficult.

The lunch finished and the bill carefully preserved for expenses, writer and art director return to their desks for a session of mental pencil sharpening. Magazines and old cop-

5 1

ies of the *Art Director's Annual* are leafed through. There are long periods of silence and gazing out of the window. An odd line is tapped out on the typewriter; a desultory scribble is made on the layout pad. To an observer, the scene has all the creative drama of two people waiting for a bus.

Every so often, the executive in charge of the account will poke his hopeful head in the door to see whether his team has been visited by the muse.

"How's it going?"

The writer and art director look up from their reference books—*Masterpieces of Erotic Photography, The Hundred Greatest Advertisements Ever Written*—and glare at the intruder. What does he think this is, a factory? Just press a button and get a campaign? Doesn't he realize that he is interrupting a most complex and delicate chain of deliberations that will ultimately lead to the great idea? How can the act of creation take place with idiots like him trampling in and out and disturbing these highly tuned brain cells? *Fuck off*.

The executive withdraws and the team resumes its pondering. At last, one of them puts forward a line or a visual idea. "What about if we . . ."

Almost before the words are spoken, they're rejected. If no other reason comes quickly to mind, there is always the old dismissive standby: It's been done before. In fact, plagiarism and the use of images and personalities that are already established in the public consciousness have often worked very well in advertising campaigns, but not this time—or at least not yet. There are still a few days to go before the deadline, before the serious panic sets in. Let's see if we can find something *really different*. (Which, translated, means: Let's see if I can find something *really different* and much better than that terrible idea of yours.) The window gazing and pencil sharpening continue.

As the days pass, the visits from the executive become more frequent and exchanges become more heated. Still nothing emerges from the temple of creativity. It is time for the trump card, which the executive delivers with some relish: The client has called the chairman of the agency and insisted on a meeting to see the new campaign, and of course the chairman has assured him that it will be ready. More than that; it will be a gem of a campaign, loved by the sales force, adored by the public, envied by the competition.

But where is it? The creative team's office is like a submarine under attack from depth charges. Every five minutes, it seems, people are coming in to nag about their own particular deadlines: The production manager needs the roughs so that he can put in hand the typesetting and finished artwork that will transform scruffy bits of paper into advertisements of presentation standard; the TV producer needs the storyboards so that the commercials can be costed and maybe rough commercials made; the executive needs to see the idea so that he can tailor the marketing evidence to support it; the planners, the researchers, and the media buyers all come and go, cursing about the impossible lack of time. The creative director, who often has the job of presenting the campaign, takes up semipermanent residence in the office, and even the chairman, conscious of his promises to the client, may hover briefly before going to lunch.

It is all very gratifying to our heroes. Now that they have succeeded in bringing most of the agency to a state of desperate expectation, they can get down to work. Social engagements are abandoned. Husbands, wives, girlfriends, boyfriends, and the bartender at "21" are made aware of the

5 3

inhuman pressure being applied. Weekends are ignored. The lights burn late. It's a brutal business, this quest for inspiration.

But when it comes, as it inevitably does in one form or another, what a satisfying change in relationships takes place. Instead of being hounded for work by every busybody in the agency, it is now the turn of the writer and art director to do the hounding. Of course roughs can be finished, commercials estimated, media and marketing plans revised, and slides and charts prepared in the space of forty-eight hours. These are mechanical tasks, nothing compared to the sweat and genius that have gone into the act of creation. Relaxed and triumphant, the writer and art director head for the local watering hole for a quiet celebration while their colleagues work on into the night.

There is barely time for a rehearsal before the day of presentation, and this is not always as useful as it might be because many of the props are still being prepared. Never mind. The presentation team is now united and optimistic. Anyone but a complete knucklehead can see that this is one of those rare campaigns that will run and run, making handsome profits for the agency and expensive reputations for its creators. The stage manager, usually the account director, goes through the order of events and checks the cues that will activate the lighting and the battery of audiovisual equipment concealed behind and around the conference room. Tomorrow is the big day, and it is awaited with nervous confidence.

It begins early, and with more panic. Despite working through the night at triple overtime, one of the studios has not quite finished putting the final gloss on some material that is absolutely vital to the presentation. Cabs and messengers crisscross the city while the account director tries to devise some plausible distraction that will delay the proceedings without making the agency look like a bunch of last-minute amateurs. Maybe the chairman could engage the senior client in some man-to-man talk about the broad canvas of industry, but what the hell are we going to do with the rest of them?

Meanwhile, the receptionist has had her copy of *Cosmopolitan* confiscated and has been reminded for the eighteenth time of the client's name. All secretaries who are likely to be visible as the visiting entourage makes its way to the conference room are given something, anything, to type so that the agency will exude an atmosphere of diligent efficiency. The reception area is double-checked for dirty ashtrays and dog-eared pornographic magazines that have been left behind by printers' reps and space salesmen. And then, not a minute too soon, the creaking, leather-clad hulk of a messenger shambles in with the missing material.

Right! We're ready for them. The agency welcoming committee can now assume the confident air of people who have never known a moment's anxiety in their lives, and the account director abandons his emergency plan for delaying the start of the presentation. The damn client will probably be late, anyway.

But, punctual to the second, the elevator doors open and a covey of young businesspeople in dark suits, led by the senior client and bristling with attaché cases, makes its purposeful way into the reception area.

There is a hasty adding up of numbers by the account director, because it is a part of presentation politesse that every member of the client's party should have an agency counterpart. Normally, the attendance figures are advised in advance, but sometimes the client will bring along a surprise guest, and the agency is obliged to find an extra body. It would never do to be caught short of one young man in a dark suit.

The seating arrangements in the conference room have been worked out with an eye for protocol that would do credit to a diplomatic banquet. The senior people from both sides are within murmuring distance of one another, and the lower ranks are paired off in less important seats. The account director opens the meeting with a few brief remarks—delighted to have the opportunity, rare to have such a thorough and helpful brief, please feel free to ask questions as we go along—and then hands it over to the agency demolition squad.

Their job is to dissect the advertising of the competition—to point out its flaws, its shaky positioning, the opportunities it has missed, the gaps it has left, the insights it has failed to perceive, the errors of execution. This is done in a detached, logical, almost scientific fashion. Vulgar jeering is carefully avoided. The tone is restrained and academic and, if it is done by experts, very effective.

Its purpose, of course, is to set the client off down the path to the inescapable conclusion that all will be revealed later on. As in other meetings, signs of encouragement are hoped for, but the senior client is professionally impassive, and the entourage is careful to follow his example. For the agency people who are on their feet trying to coax a glimmer of sympathetic response from the audience, it is like preaching to zombies. But they plow on with their slides and charts and statistical analyses and meticulously supported assumptions until the background has been well and truly filled in and the moment of truth arrives: The campaign, in all its ingenious manifestations, is about to be exposed.

Academic observations now give way to something akin to cabaret. The agency's best presenter, redolent with charm, produces one great ad after another as though he were pulling rabbits out of a hat. Jingles are played through the conference room's sound system at a volume just bearable to the human ear. TV commercials, rough but promising, appear on the screen. Evidence of creative effort comes bursting out of the walls, and all that is missing is someone jumping out of a giant cake. (Although even this, if the client is a cake manufacturer, can't be ruled out.)

At the end, as the conference room's lights come up and the best presenter sits down, the agency people look expectantly at the client people, modest smiles of achievement on their faces, not expecting applause, perhaps, but eager for some token of appreciation.

The senior client, however, is not to be rushed. There is no chance that he will flout years of tradition by expressing his own opinion before he has put his young colleagues through their paces, and the most junior of these is told to share his thoughts with the attentive group around the table. Notes are consulted. A throat is cleared. The young man is not quite sure whether to address his remarks to his boss or to the agency chairman, and even less sure of what those remarks ought to be. In the chasm between unqualified enthusiasm and outright rejection lies the prudent course to take, but there should be some hint somewhere of a point of view, otherwise he's going to look like a dunce, incapable of constructive thought and therefore not senior-executive material.

He starts safely enough: "The agency's approach is very interesting, and they have clearly devoted a lot of time and effort in coming to their conclusions."

So far, so good. Now for the tricky part, with everyone hanging on his words—the agency, to see whether he will be a useful ally or a difficult little creep; his colleagues,

57

to see if this first straw in the wind seems to be blowing in an acceptable direction; his boss, sitting inscrutably at the top of the table—they are all waiting, watching, pencils poised over notepads. Oh, God.

He takes a flying leap toward the middle of the road. "On the one hand, the agency's ideas are undoubtedly . . . well, *interesting*." (*Fresh* and *different* can also be used here without too much risk.) "And there are some aspects of the campaign that would probably work very well, although obviously they're still rough and would need to be discussed in detail and researched and fine-tuned." (An invaluably vague word, *fine-tuned*.) "On the other hand, there is a possibility—only a possibility—that certain requirements set out in the brief have been, if not exactly neglected, not given sufficient emphasis."

Before he can be pinned to the wall by the agency and asked precisely what he means, he sprints toward a summing-up. "The one hand" and "the other hand" having been used, "in general" is now the only phrase that has the necessary air of finality without having sufficient weight to cause the speaker to lose his balance and fall off the fence. "In general, therefore, the agency has come up with some very interesting proposals, and it would be very . . . well . . . interesting to see how they plan to develop them."

More of this goes on, sometimes hours of it, until the senior client is ready to unburden himself. By this time, the agency people are leaning forward like young cuckoos waiting for a worm. Surely now there will be a decisive and favorable response, followed by champagne in the chairman's office, banner headlines in the trade press, and another few million to add to the agency's billings. The anticipation is excruciating.

The senior client chooses his words as if he were selecting a cigar; he hasn't gotten where he is by blurting out his opinion without first making a few suitably statesmanlike remarks. And so he thanks the agency for its efforts, perhaps with a wry reference to midnight oil, before picking his way through the comments that have been made in the course of the presentation. The agency fidgets. Is he going to buy it? Do we get the worm? For heaven's sake, man, get on with it.

And he does, but very rarely in the definitive way that the agency is hoping for.

"All I am prepared to say at the moment is that you have given us a great deal—a great deal—to think about." He looks at the agency chairman and smiles a tycoon-to-tycoon smile. "I'm sure you weren't expecting an instant decision when there are so many considerations to take into account."

An instant decision is exactly what the agency chairman, an optimist to his toenails, *was* expecting, but he does his best to be a tycoon about it, nodding sagely as he tries to avoid thinking about the enormous amount of money that has just been spent to achieve an anticlimax.

Souvenirs are distributed—inch-thick marketing documents stuffed with statistics and conclusions, decorated with miniature reproductions of advertisements and storyboards and "personalized" with potted biographies of the agency personnel who would work on the account. Once the client party has been escorted out of the agency, the presentation team returns to the conference room for the postmortem. The clients and their reactions are discussed and analyzed, and the odd recrimination is voiced about somebody's lackluster presentation performance, but it's all inconclusive and often rather depressing. There's nothing to be done now except wait for the client's verdict, and the bastard didn't even give a hint about when that might be.

Normal service in the agency is resumed, and those tasks, great and small, that were neglected or postponed during the panic are picked up again in a rash of meetings.

The writer and art director who worked on the presentation are feeling an even greater sense of deflation than the rest of the agency. They sweated blood. They produced a masterpiece of persuasive communication, and what happened? *It wasn't sold properly.* Another black mark on the record of their executive colleagues, more ammunition in the cold war between the princes of creativity and the rest of the world. Fortunately, they can now divert themselves with a job that has been dragging on for many months and that is at last ready for execution: their epic commercial.

The average cost of a thirty-second commercial, without anything too complicated in the way of special optical effects, is at least $250,000. If a celebrity is used, there is a considerable fee on top of that, plus handsome repeat fees every time the commercial is shown. Prime-time television costs approximately $100,000 a minute. With an investment of this size, it is not hard to see why the progress of most commercials, from original concept to finished film, is slow and often extremely frustrating.

It was months ago that the writer and art director labored and brought forth their idea, drawn up on a storyboard. The creative director approved it, the account people accepted it, and it was gradually sold up through the levels of client management. It was generally agreed that the commercial was on strategy, but the client had some misgivings about the details of execution, and so it was put into research.

The original storyboard was drawn up again, in more

finished form. A sound track of commentary and music was recorded and the elements were put together to make a film—still rough but sufficiently clear for a representative selection of the target audience (possibly those long-suffering housewives from Queens) to understand and comment on it. A screening was arranged, and the housewives were invited to see the preview of a new television show. During the screening, they were also treated to a sight of the new commercial, and among the questions they were asked afterward were questions about the commercial.

At this point, complications set in, because research people are not satisfied with simple answers. It is not enough to know that Mrs. Jones liked the commercial. How *much* did she like it, on a scale of one to ten? What did she remember? Was there anything in the commercial she disliked? Would she be: (a) very interested in trying the product? (b) quite interested in trying the product? (c) not interested in trying the product? Reams of completed questionnaires are then studied and analyzed. The results, which are always open to considerable interpretation, are worried over and inspected from different angles by the agency and the client. Weeks pass, but eventually qualified approval is given and the show can go on.

Meanwhile, the writer, the art director, and the agency producer have been hard at lunch, deciding various artistic matters, and at the top of their list is the choice of director.

At the end of 1989, there were 464 directors of TV commercials in London chasing barely three thousand commercials and revised versions. Competition as keen as this breeds specialists, and so there are directors who specialize in dialogue, in fashion, in action, in special effects, in hair, in drinks, in any one of a dozen subdivisions of technique. But for our agency trio, putting together their epic, these worthy craftsmen are not quite what they had in mind, not *heavy-weight* enough. They are united in their desire to get a features director who is resting between engagements.

It comes as a surprise to many people to discover that internationally known film directors are often more than happy to descend from their artistic eminence to shoot a commercial. What is it that lures them away from Gene Hackman in Hollywood to an unknown character actor in New York? How can a commercial for a soft drink compare with the creative scope offered by a tale of love and violence on the big screen?

The reason, in one form or another, is money—not just the director's fee (although that has been known to reach $30,000 a day) but the luxury of time and the size of the production budgets, which, in relative terms, are infinitely more generous than those allocated to feature films.

Instead of breaking his neck to get five or ten minutes of usable film in the can every day, all the director has to worry about is thirty or forty seconds. And the money available for production values—the props and all those barely glimpsed but wonderful touches that make set designers twitch in ecstasy—is there by the bucketful: *four thousand dollars a second*. This gives a director the chance to make a small but perfect thing, a marvelously polished tiny film that will not only keep his hand in but will also go some way toward helping with the alimony payments.

The agency producer makes his calls to Los Angeles to see who might be free to consider the commercial. Scripts are sent out and timetables are juggled. The first of many budget battles takes place when the true cost of the director's involvement is calculated—his air fares, his board and lodging, his five-figure daily rate, and his well-known habit of shooting into the night on overtime—but these are small concerns when compared with the awards that will mark this as one of the legendary, never-to-be-forgotten commercials.

Once the director has been recruited, daily contact with the agency producer is maintained by the director's producer, who will be in charge of organizing the set, the crew, the equipment, the money, the catering, and a hundred other details that have to be seen to. In addition, and most important of all, the director must be kept happy. He is the star, and he must not be bothered by trifles. In other words, the producer is responsible for everything except the success of the commercial, credit for which is shared between the director and the agency people.

As one might expect, the road to the shoot is paved with meetings. There are preproduction meetings, casting sessions, auditions, lunches, drinks, budget adjustments— sometimes with the client, as often as possible without him. The director's presence is used sparingly, because we don't want him to be upset by a twit of a brand manager who keeps insisting on a ten-second product shot in the middle of the commercial. That little problem is swept under the carpet, to be argued about when the rough cut is ready.

On the day of the shoot, a small army converges on the studio's soundstage. The agency people, after an unsuccessful struggle, have been obliged to bring the client. There might easily be a crew of twenty or more, for sound, lighting, camera operating, focus pulling, makeup, hairdressing, catering, each with jealously guarded areas of expertise. Woe betide the helpful continuity person who happens to be standing by a light that the camera operator wants moved three inches to the left. If she attempts to move it, the electricians will be up in arms.

There will be the artistes, studying the script next to

63

the sound crew, who are studying page three of the *Daily News*. There will be the producer and a personal assistant. And there will be that lordly figure dressed in crumpled but expensive clothing, the director.

Now that everyone has arrived, the first coffee break of the day can be taken. Doughnuts and croissants are distributed, and the crew stands around chatting about last week's job, when, due to the director's upset stomach, they ran into considerable and lucrative overtime, which they refer to affectionately as the diarrhea bonus.

For the client, who has never attended the shooting of a commercial before, it is disappointingly matter-of-fact. This is, after all, a *film*. Where is the drama, the electric atmosphere before a great performance, the *glamour?*

Little does he know, at 8:30 in the morning, that his most enduring memory of the day will be one of boredom, often accompanied by heartburn caused by bad coffee and too many sugary treats. His hours on the set will be hours of immense tedium and discomfort. He will not be allowed to speak or move while the camera is turning. He will hold himself unnaturally still, fighting off cramps, and peer toward the center of activity in the hope of seeing something exciting, because here he is on the fringes of show business. Those are real actors. That is a real director. Something exciting *must* happen.

And what does he see? The same short sequence repeated ten, fifteen, twenty times. Dialogue that was amusing at ten o'clock is irritating by eleven and actively offensive by noon. And it all sounds identical, anyway. Why go through it again?

Because, unknown to a novice like him who doesn't know a whip pan from a lap dissolve, there is *always* some slight imperfection, perceptible only to the director's merci-less eye and hypercritical ear.

TAKE ONE: The actor delivers his lines superbly, but someone in the darkest corner of the set shuffled his feet and the sound engineer has picked up the shuffle on the tape.

TAKE TWO: The actor delivers his lines superbly, but the makeup artist notices a drop of perspiration on the side of his nose.

TAKE THREE: The nose stays dry, but the actor doesn't quite repeat his previous superb delivery.

And so it goes on. And on. And on. There are frequent pauses for refreshment after the first coffee break—the early lunch break, the disturbed lunch break, the afternoon break, the preovertime break—and it is possible to eat rather badly five or six times in the course of the day. It is the proud boast of the film technicians' union that it has never in its history lost a member through lack of nourishment.

The shooting day starts at about eight and ends when the director is satisfied, which may unusually be as early as five or as late as the budget can stand the overtime. At the end of it, there will be an hour or so of film from which to choose the magic thirty seconds. The rough cut will be the subject of further meetings and more editing. The brand manager will want his ten-second product shot. The agency and the production company will resist. And the director will be on the plane back to Los Angeles, having made sure that his preferred cut of the commercial, which may or may

65

not bear any resemblance to the final film, is put on his personal show reel.

It has been a taxing experience for all concerned, but as everyone in advertising agrees, it's a tough business. People outside it have no idea what we have to go through. *Have another drink.*

Pigs with Checkbooks

Even with a kindly and forgiving eye, it is difficult to select from the millions of advertising messages on display at any one time more than a handful with any original merit. These are the famous advertisements and campaigns, the work that is remembered and liked, the work that sells products and services with wit and charm and imagination. Triumphs such as these are held up, quite rightly, as examples of what advertising should be, but they are rare. A very generous estimate might put the incidence of good or brilliant advertising as high as 10 percent of the overall output. The rest is dross.

The rest is either boring, derivative, strident (when in doubt, shout), offensively stupid, patronizing, or so smug that the most mild-mannered consumer could be forgiven for being provoked to physical violence. There is a limit to the number of times anyone can endure the sight of plastic middle-class couples gloating over their new cars, sipping their sticky after-dinner drinks, or going into raptures over a thin, mean liquid that masquerades as coffee.

We are often told that advertising reflects the face of society, which would be extremely depressing if it was wholly true. Nearer the truth is that advertising reflects the face of the client. He is the first member of the public outside the agency to judge an advertising idea. He can approve it, tinker with it, or kill it and demand something worse because, as he will point out if faced with too much argument, he's paying for it. "Just remember it's our money you're spending here" is a phrase that has hung ominously over many a conference table, and it is enough to make most agencies back off and do what they're told.

As you would expect, agencies do not enjoy this situation. It is not comfortable to live with. But, ingenious to the last, they have developed a philosophy that enables them to take the money and duck the issue at the same time. Expressed in simple terms, it is the whiskery old excuse that clients get the advertising they deserve, which conveniently ignores the option that agencies can always take against nightmare accounts and their attendant goon squads. They can resign the business. They seldom do.

To provide themselves with some daily consolation, agency people take pleasure in devising new and ever more derogatory ways of describing their tormentors—"pigs with checkbooks" being one of the more moderate phrases in a litany of invective and profanity that is muttered (out of the client's hearing, naturally) in agency offices throughout the world.

It would be tempting to dismiss this as nothing more than the harmless grumbling of an oppressed minority group, but we would be wrong to do so. While all clients do not automatically qualify as the subhuman morons that agencies claim them to be, there are enough suspect characters in the client population to justify many of the accusations that are made against them. Since clients themselves are lovers of labels and pigeonholes, it is appropriate to label and pigeonhole them here.

The Agency's Pal

This is usually a brand manager who finds the environment of an agency much more to his taste than his own modest surroundings in the suburbs. He likes the slightly racy nature of agency people and makes a point of cultivating the writer and art director so that he can feel he's up there in the front line, on the cutting edge of the creative process. He likes the secretaries, who tend to be prettier and more respectful than the women in his office. He likes the lunches. He lives in hope that one day he might be permitted to go off on location (with lavish expenses) when the agency team shoots the next commercial in the Bahamas. And, quite often, he has ambitions to change sides and become a racy advertising person himself.

He is never in a hurry to go back to the suburbs when the meeting is over. Instead, he loiters in the agency, friendly and admiring, until eventually he is adopted as an ally, a good guy, a client who is human.

This testing time comes when a new campaign is presented to his god and master, the marketing director. Our pal has been closely involved in the campaign, and he has

69

been unwise enough to tell the agency, over another three-hour lunch at Luigi's, that he thinks it's great. He's committed. Terrific! The campaign's as good as sold.

But the marketing director, resplendent in his expensive silk tie and rather less expensive suit, is not happy with the campaign. He looks down his nose and shakes his head. He has concerns, grave concerns. Oh dear.

The agency looks to its pal for support. Does he stand up and pound the table and argue passionately for the campaign? Does he repeat those words of praise and encouragement that flowed as profusely as wine during lunch last week? Does he come out fighting? Does he, hell. He is bent over his notes, avoiding eye contact with his old cronies, nodding in agreement as the marketing director drones on. He is no longer the *agency's pal*. He has reverted to type. He's a client.

The Eunuch in the Harem

There are two characteristics that identify this particular pest. The first is a reflex action: As a script or a piece of copy is presented to him, he produces his gold pen and holds it poised over the paper like the scalpel of a surgeon about to remove a malignant growth. After a few moments of slashing and scribbling, he looks up with a rueful smile and a sigh, as though he has just averted a disaster. Here comes the second characteristic:

"Well, I'm no copywriter, but I think I've made some improvements." He slides the defaced text across to the account executive and sits back. God, sometimes you have to do everything yourself.

He's quite right, in fact. He is no copywriter. He

70

can't even write a short, lucid letter. His "improvements" are gobbledygook, great chunks lifted straight out of the marketing strategy and dropped on the page like dead mice. The agency may duck and dive, but to no avail. He won't allow a word to be changed. He is bursting with the pride of authorship. He has written an advertisement.

A variation is sometimes slipped into this performance in the shape of "my wife." She has been shown or told about the new campaign, and she is unimpressed. Her opinion carries considerable weight because of her dual qualifications in the matter of judging advertising: She is not only "my wife" but she is a housewife, too, and therefore possesses some secret knowledge denied to the rest of us.

At least in this case the agency is not obliged to accept gibberish verbatim, but the revised brief from "my wife" is impossibly vague and causes much discussion in the creative department.

All this springs from the widely held view that any fool can write copy, which is partly true. Any fool can write bad copy, and many fools do.

The Thug

He acts the part of a bluff, no-nonsense man of the people, too shrewd to be manipulated by a slick bunch of kids with marketing degrees, whom he invariably addresses as "you admen." "Don't play any games with me," he says. "I like the straight-talking, direct approach. I call a spade a spade."

This may initially be quite refreshing, but it is not a reciprocal arrangement. He can and does call a spade a spade, often using blunt and insulting language to do so. But should the agency take this as a cue to respond in the same way, the bluff veneer disappears and the thug is revealed, a crude bully who will not tolerate argument and who uses his advertising budget like a cattle prod.

He likes to make his agency jump, and he doesn't bother with any of the conventional forms of commercial politeness. He will call up on Tuesday night to summon the agency to an out-of-town breakfast meeting on Wednesday. And then, just to show who's boss, he'll be late. He will demand complicated revisions to commercials, revisions that must be done in twenty-four hours so that he can see them before he leaves the city, and then refuse to approve the overtime bills. "You should have gotten it right the first time," he'll say. "That's what I'm paying you for."

When he visits the agency, he treats it as his personal domain, using secretaries to make his dinner reservations, to go out and buy his cigars, to get his theater tickets, to confirm his travel arrangements, and to order his limos. Curiously, for such an important man, he never seems to have any money with him to pay for these small services. If anyone has the audacity to suggest reimbursement, he will fix them with his bully's stare and mention the vast profits that the agency is making from his business.

He likes loud, aggressive advertising. Any attempts at subtlety are dismissed with a sneer as being too clever by half (one of his favorite bluff, no-nonsense expressions). He assumes that the public, like his agency, can be browbeaten into submission. If the agency should dare to dig its heels in, he will unveil his secret weapon: a man he plays golf with every weekend who runs a small provincial agency and who would be delighted to take over the account and bellow to order.

Thugs are common in advertising and always will be.

For every agency prepared to throw them out, there are half a dozen others willing to pocket their self-respect along with the commission.

The Man with the Outstretched Hand

A certain amount of petty bribery exists in any business, whether it's described as entertainment, oiling the wheels of commerce, or a token to mark the sincere appreciation of a wonderful working relationship. The odd case of champagne, the days at the track, the evenings at the Met—these are all considered perfectly harmless and acceptable.

But it doesn't always stop there, because every once in a while (rarely, it's true) the agency will find itself dealing with a client on the take. He won't be the top man in the client organization, but he covets the top man's salary, the top man's suits, and the top man's car. He knows to a penny how much the agency is making from his business, and he will start referring to it more and more often during those informal chats at the end of the working day.

At the same time, he will drop wistful and very clear hints about some desirable object he can't afford. If the agency man is sufficiently alert and naïve, the hint will be picked up and the desirable object will be given as a Christmas present. After all, he's an amiable client (they always are) and it is a good, profitable account.

But the hints don't stop. They become more blatant and demanding, and the naïve agency man begins to realize that he and the agency are being blackmailed. Either the presents keep coming or the client will initiate an agency review, and we can imagine what that means. No need to spell it out, old boy. I think we both know where we stand.

7 ³

The agency can report the man to his boss, possibly ruining his career or losing the business. Or it can continue to pay the squeeze, which will become progressively more severe: After the TV set and the stereo equipment, there might be two or three Armani suits, airline tickets, and a new Volvo. It has also been known for a child's tuition to be taken care of in order to cement the bond between client and agency.

Of course it's dishonest and stupid. But it can be so gradual and insidious, when practiced by an expert in the art of the backhander, that an agency can be compromised while it is still trying to decide what to do. And where do you draw the line between the acceptable and the unacceptable? The difference in cost between a case of champagne and a car is enormous. The difference in principle is not that easy to measure. A man once asked a beautiful woman if she would sleep with him for a million dollars. She agreed. When he reduced his offer to five dollars, she was outraged. Did he think she was a prostitute? "Madam, that principle is already established," said the man. "All we're discussing now is the price."

The Good Client

Yes, he is out there somewhere. He is reasonable, receptive, and intelligent. He assumes that his agency has skills that his company does not have, and he is happy to work with people rather than dictate to them. He has his opinions, but he's prepared to discuss them and is not afraid of changing them if a valid argument for change is presented to him. He doesn't require lunch every time he meets the agency, he doesn't pass the buck, and he's honest.

One of the best of the good clients I've known, Anthony Simmonds-Gooding, was in charge of the Heineken account when it was small beer. He approved and stayed with a campaign that is still running after thirteen years, winning awards, helping to increase sales every year, and becoming a part of the language.

He got the advertising he deserved. It sometimes happens.

Growing Pains

The three young men whom we last met as they were planning their new agency have prospered. Their bank loan has been paid off and they have a long lease on some breathtakingly stark office space. Their client list is a mixture of small, high-visibility accounts, including an adventurous wine merchant and an aggressive charity, a solid assortment of medium-sized but growing brands, and a couple of blue-chip names. Their work is considered highly creative, and their billings this year will pass $40 million. They are profitable, well established, and dissatisfied.

The problem is that they now find themselves on the advertising plateau. Their growth rate has slowed down after the rush of early successes. They are past the days of being known as a hot young agency but still a long way off from being big enough to compete with the international monsters. And, almost worst of all, their neighbors on the plateau are all those dreary agencies they used to sneer at—the plodders who somehow manage to hang on to their clients every year despite their pedestrian campaigns and middle-aged reputations, the agencies that will never really make it. The very thought of being in the same league as they are is enough to make you rush out and order a flame-red Ferrari just to show the world that you're not pedestrian and middle-aged and gray.

Life on the plateau brings other, more insidious problems than the cooling of a hot image. The agency's metabolism has slowed down now that those initial adrenaline-inducing worries of failure and bankruptcy have been left behind. It is taken for granted that there will be a steady improvement in everybody's personal circumstances: raises and bonuses, cars and promotions. And once these are taken for granted, it is only human nature to want more. Other people in other agencies are getting more. Maybe it would be worth taking a nibble at the grass on the other side of the fence.

Accompanying these stirrings of unrest is often a certain complacency, which shows itself in different ways according to position and salary level. Junior members of the agency arrive later in the office and leave earlier for the health club. The middle ranks take longer lunches and conduct their affairs on expenses, while the top people cultivate top people's hobbies and interests. These will vary: collecting art, buying shares in racehorses, or acquiring country houses—the only common factor being that they cost enough money to necessitate substantial personal loans,

77

which will influence the agency's decision-making process in the years to come as the interest payments bite deeper and deeper.

For the three proprietors of the agency, there is a sense of limited achievement, which becomes more limited as time goes by. After all their hard work, they're sitting on a moderately successful medium-sized agency that is in danger of losing its edge. Life is comfortable enough, but they don't have any real money. And to get into the big league, where billings are a billion dollars or more, could take *forever*. (In advertising, this is a period that exceeds five years.) What is to be done to regain the momentum of the agency and to make its founders the rich men they deserve to be?

There are four options.

The first, to carry on with renewed vigor and build the agency over the next ten or twenty years into a colossus, is dismissed without much discussion. It's not quick enough.

The second is to go public. Given Wall Street's current fascination with advertising, this might be possible despite the agency's relative youth and its comparatively modest profits, and the money would certainly be useful to pay off the mortgage on the place in the Hamptons. But there wouldn't be enough to make a real fuck-everybody killing, and there would be some long and restrictive service contracts. On the whole, it wouldn't be that much better than the first option.

The third choice is to take over another agency—a nice sleepy old agency with its own office building—and leap from medium to big overnight before going public on the back of the combined profits and assets. A perfect solution, except for two major snags: Taking over another agency requires more resources than our three young men can raise without signing away their lives, and in any case there is nothing left to take over. The Saatchis and their ilk have been out shopping for years, and there are no more bargains available.

This leaves one last option, and it looks increasingly attractive as the possibilities are explored. It is to be taken over by a bigger agency, but taken over only in a technical sense. The practical result would be a reverse takeover, with the three young men ending up on the top of the heap.

Obviously, the victim must be chosen with great care. It has to be an agency that knows it lacks what the young men can provide: a reputation for good creative work. It has to have a base of docile clients who won't stampede as soon as the new regime moves in. And, ideally, it should have tired or soggy management that won't offer much of a struggle over the transference of power.

At any given time, there are always two or three agencies around that more or less meet these requirements. Advertising is a business that demands constant enthusiasm from top management. When this flags, the agency starts to wallow, and without an injection of fresh blood, it will eventually lose clients and staff. It has happened a hundred times, and has provided a hundred opportunities for the kind of maneuver that the young men are now planning with such excitement. The adrenaline is back! It's like the old days, except that the potential rewards can now be measured in millions.

The publicly known facts about the likely agencies are studied. One of them seems to be sufficiently moribund, and its client list is analyzed to see whether there would be any serious areas of conflict between brands or companies. It would be miraculous, for instance, if their disposable diaper client was to stay with the merged agencies once we'd arrived with our disposable diaper client. And so client lists

79

are compared, only superficially at this stage, to see whether they mesh.

Once it looks as though the two agencies could be put together without any significant client defections, the next step is to make contact with the victim agency's owners to get an idea of their levels of interest, competence, greed, ambition, and usefulness. (Occasionally, the first overture is made by the victims, who have seen the writing on the agency's wall and who are looking for a comfortable retirement. This can save a lot of time and lunch bills.)

A drink is suggested in a suitably quiet bar, somewhere that requires a tie and is thus unlikely to be full of other advertising people, and the preliminary circling begins. Each side is at great pains to be flattering about the other side's agency, and under the cover of small talk there is an almost-audible whir of brains as personalities are assessed to see how things might work out in the event of a deal. If each side is hopeful that it can get what it wants out of the arrangement, whether power or money or an important and well-paid but undemanding title, the meeting ends on a cordial and promising note: We must talk again soon.

And talk they do, in greater and greater detail, at lunches and dinners held in progressively more secretive circumstances. It might spoil everything if the cat was to jump out of the bag before the clients had been primed, and so private suites are booked in hotels and enormous trouble is taken to keep well away from prying eyes and flapping ears, which is not at all easy in the advertising business. This search for the totally discreet table was once taken to extremes by the principals in a deal involving two London agencies; they decided that the only safe place to have lunch was Miami.

The greatest imponderable, chewed over endlessly, is

how the clients are going to take to the news of their chosen agency getting into bed with a bunch of strangers. While the merger will be presented as a marriage made in heaven that will benefit absolutely everybody ("complementary areas of expertise, greater depth of management, improved creative resources"), it would be wildly optimistic, even by advertising standards, to assume a zero casualty rate. But how many clients will feel that their noses have been put out of joint? How many can be soothed into a state of acceptance? How many will decline the advances of other agencies that will be made as soon as the merger is announced? Conjecture can go on indefinitely, but conjecture is no substitute for action. You have to try it and see.

A lesser imponderable is the reaction of the staff. Some will stay and some will go, but, unlike clients, they are at least subject to some forms of control, and most of them are susceptible to inducements of one kind or another to keep them in line. Nevertheless, it's a problem. When two fully staffed agencies get together, there are two sets of everyone. To make financial sense of the merger, the combined payroll will probably have to be cut by a minimum of 25 percent. Naturally, each agency is reluctant to sacrifice its own people, sometimes out of loyalty and a genuine belief in the abilities of its staff, sometimes out of a crude instinct for self-preservation: If we outnumber them, my personal position is likely to be stronger.

But before the haggling over staff can begin, there are two matters of the utmost importance and delicacy to be decided, so fundamental that lack of agreement can bring the cozy negotiations to a sudden and permanent halt.

The two are closely linked, and the first is the choice of a name for the new agency. There are many possibilities here, since each agency is bringing to the merger its own precious collection of names or initials; the combined total will never be fewer than four, and it could be as many as eight. The logical solution, one might think, would be to string them together in alphabetical order and get on with something more important, but that seldom happens. The order of the names and initials is crucial because it is a public statement about who is in charge of the merged agency. Also, everyone involved in the merger is experienced enough to know the fate that lies in store for the names on the end of the list: dropped from daily speech and relegated to the letterhead.

No wonder the atmosphere is charged as the nettle is tentatively grasped: "Has anyone had any thoughts about the name?"

Yes indeed. Marvels of self-interested invention are put forward to support the view that the other side's name should come last. If it happens to suit the argument, even alphabetical order—"It's so much easier for people to remember"—might be tried. But that can always be countered by another, equally suspect assumption: "Our clients wouldn't be happy." (Agencies like to believe that clients share their preoccupation with names.)

In fact, this stage of the negotiations is interesting, and the final decision revealing, because it reflects the result of the first trial of strength between the two sets of management—the first of many accommodations that will be made by the weaker side in deference to the stronger. One side always needs the merger more than the other, and the degree of need can usually be measured by the concessions that are made, not only in agreeing on the name but in the jockeying for status that follows.

Two chairmen, two managing directors, two creative directors, two financial directors: There is an entire corporate Noah's Ark to be reshuffled and retitled, and it is damn tricky work. Joint titles won't do, since nobody takes them seriously, and there is a limit to the number of labels available in any single hierarchy. But all is not lost, because here, a sop to many an ego, the inspired notion of a holding company comes into its own, with all its multifarious divisions: International, Acquisitions & Development, Public Relations, Communications Studies, Management Consultancy—a brave new world as yet uninhabited by a single executive. Surely room can be found in this exciting and infinitely elastic structure for the overflow from the agency boardroom.

And, in due course, it is. All that remains to be decided now is the allocation of shares, which prompts one final round of bartering, and then the new, improved agency can concentrate on preparing as seductive a marriage announcement as possible.

The content of these announcements is fairly standard. Better everything is promised—better service, better creative work, better media buying—and the joining together of the two agencies is presented as the most natural of developments, inspired by the deep admiration that each agency has for the other. Somewhere in the announcement will be a quote along the following lines: "The more we looked into it, the more it made sense to consolidate our abilities and resources so that we could offer a broader range of expertise in today's increasingly competitive business climate." It's simple, harmless stuff, and none but the most gullible would be misled by it for a moment.

The timing of the announcement is not quite so easy. The more important clients will already have been sounded out, but they are not necessarily any more discreet than agency people, and it would be embarrassing if one of them

8 3

leaked the news prematurely. *Ad Age* would get hold of it and bellow about merger rumors, the poor ignorant staff would get jittery, the uninformed clients would be upset, and other agencies would be on to them quicker than you could say conflict of interest.

So, in a last-minute frenzy of phone calls and assignations, the news is given out to everyone within one frantic twenty-four-hour period. The staff is told that golden opportunities lie ahead, clients are given the party line, *Ad Age* is offered a limited exclusive, press releases are sent by messenger to influential journalists, champagne is served in the boardroom, and photographs are taken of the beaming newlyweds.

Then the problems begin. Having declared their intentions, the two agencies have to move in together. Those stark offices aren't big enough, and so for the time being everyone is jammed into less fashionable accommodations while new premises are found, gutted, and redesigned. The staff is cramped and apprehensive. They know that any day now the "consolidation of resources" will make a good many of them redundant. Friends in other agencies are sounded out in case another job has to be found in a hurry, and uneasy speculation takes up much of the time that used to be devoted to work.

The management, however, is working fourteen hours a day. The merger will not be considered successful unless it is blessed fairly quickly by the arrival of more business, and this is unlikely to happen if too many of the existing clients take exception to the new arrangement and leave. It is a hectic two or three months of keeping one set of masters happy while courting another, and it is not made any easier by the friction within the agency caused by overcrowding and political skirmishes.

The creative people can be counted on to make a meal out of the situation. They find that they can't concentrate in unfamiliar surroundings. They are not pleased to be reporting to a different creative director, and the executives they are now being asked to work with are, if anything, even worse than the last bunch of idiots. They accuse the management of selling out, of letting creative standards drop, of kissing the client's ass. They feel slighted, almost betrayed. They mope.

The executives tend to take a more businesslike view, seeing opportunities for advancement in the increased size of the agency. But the creative department, suspicious and touchy though it may be, is not their chief concern. The hand in need of holding at the moment is the client's hand, because he is definitely feeling a little insecure. He, too, might have been demoted in the merger from being one of the old agency's big clients to one of the new agency's medium-sized clients. Is he still going to receive the service and attention that he is used to? Can he look forward to a continuation of his pleasant relationship with the creative director, those unhurried chats about the size of the logo or the sound track on the latest commercial? Will there still be those agreeable dinners with the chairman two or three times a year? Will he still be loved?

Yes, yes, says the executive, massaging furiously, of course he will. Clients like him are the backbone of the agency, and together we will grow. Onward and upward! How about lunch next week? (Agency mergers are always wonderful for the restaurant business.) And yet, despite all the protestations of goodwill and confidence, there is a wait-and-see atmosphere. The client may admit it or he may keep it to himself, but he is reserving judgment.

This is not lost on the rest of the advertising industry,

and the poachers are sharpening their knives and forks with a vengeance. The months immediately following a merger are assumed, with some justification, to be a period during which stirrings of discontent can be converted to advantage, and it is a rare merger client who doesn't receive daily offers of food and drink and speculative presentations from agencies he has never met and often never heard of.

Meanwhile, the consolidation of abilities and resources at Merger House is taking place. The unlucky ones are paid off and asked to take their personal effects and hurt feelings elsewhere as quickly as possible. They're not expected to work out their periods of notice; on the contrary, they're encouraged not to, since to have people under sentence of death hanging around the agency is considered bad for morale.

For the ones who remain, particularly those who have been rewarded in one way or another, the merger begins to look like quite a good idea, after all. The agency has accelerated off the plateau and up into a different league. There are bigger and better opportunities at every level, and if they can be properly exploited, everyone will benefit. Fame and fortune are just around the corner, and once the agency has settled into its imposing new offices, a lot of the initial friction will disappear. A change of surroundings often works wonders in dispelling the prickly atmosphere of those first uncomfortable weeks.

In the end, most of the clients wait to see how things turn out. They may have misgivings, but their instinct is to stay put. Changing agencies is hard work, time-consuming, and disruptive, and the devil you know is usually preferred over the devil you don't. Providing the agency is careful to maintain as much continuity as possible and to put on its most enthusiastic face, the misgivings should be forgotten.

The three men have almost pulled it off. The board is not entirely obedient (no board ever is), but the deadwood has been cleared out and the client list hasn't suffered too badly. The merger has been 90 percent successful; a big piece of new business would add the final 10 percent, and then they can start planning their assault on the Stock Exchange. How difficult can that be? It's only another variation of the new business pitch.

Invasion of the Men in Suits

At one time, not all that long ago, it was almost inconceivable that the denizens of Wall Street and the City of London could consider advertising worthy of shareholders' attention. Agencies were regarded as entertaining, good at lunch, even useful, but slightly suspect, run and staffed by unpredictable people who were quite likely to argue with their clients and often had the impertinence to insist that they knew best. And who could say for sure that they didn't? As the first Lord Leverhulme complained: "Half the money I spend on advertising is wasted, and the trouble is I don't know which half."

There are two responses to the attitude that prompts remarks like that. One is to admit that advertising is an inexact business and probably always will be, but this is not an admission that will encourage confidence in either clients or investors.

The other response is to surround the central function of the agency, producing advertising, with an elaborate range of supporting services in order to get as far away as possible from the bad old days of the idea salesman and into the position of the total communications consultant, a purveyor of top-level advice rather than a lowly supplier of words and pictures.

Not surprisingly, most agencies have chosen the second option, and over the last few years some have done it remarkably well, elevating the status of the industry to such an extent that the traders now look with interest at any agency that feels the itch to go public. No wonder our three young men—by now, it's true, not quite so young—are confident that they will soon be in there rubbing shoulders with the other members of the advertising millionaires' club.

Before that can happen, however, they must learn to package themselves for the merchant bankers, the financial journalists, and the assorted investment consultants who make up their target audience, and their first lesson is this: Good figures alone are not enough. Wall Street has to feel that the agency is a serious business with long-term growth prospects, run by a team of responsible and intelligent people, old heads on young shoulders, steady fellows who will ensure that the shareholders' interests are paramount.

Some minor physical modifications are necessary here in order to make the principal company assets, the management, look as attractive as possible to the punters. Personal appearance assumes a greater significance than before. The untamed hairstyles, leather jackets, and boots that were so appropriate in the dynamic, slightly antiestablishment days will have to go. Wall Street likes suits, although these can be

89

from Armani or one of the less stuffy designers. It also likes ties, once the badge of the gray plodder, but at least a hint of individuality can be retained by wearing a spotted bow tie, which has the additional advantage of being highly telegenic.

The more flamboyant aspects of behavior and personality will need a little attention, too, and any tendencies to rant or to say *fuck* every other word will have to be controlled. The editor of the *Wall Street Journal* would not be amused. In fact, the whole of one's public face has to be looked at with the same critical care that is devoted to the image of a politician seeking election. But this is not a problem. It is just presentation, and presentation is advertising's stock-in-trade.

The other disciplines and requirements involved in a public offering are a little more onerous, and perhaps the most tiresome of them all is to give the books an overhaul so that they conform to the rigid standards of fiscal probity demanded by the financial world. The agency's detailed financial records will be exposed to close inspection, and some of the old carefree habits might cause raised eyebrows among the underwriters.

The garage bills, for example, might seem a little excessive. Does a company doing business in the city really need thirty-four BMWs, six Porches, eight Jeep Cherokees, three large Mercedes, and a Maserati in addition to a cab bill of several thousand dollars a month? Is it simple coincidence that the agency retains a catering consultant who happens to be the chairman's wife? Was the boat in Florida always used for entertaining clients, even on that abortive and uncomfortable run to the Bahamas that ended so expensively with a broken mainmast? Who is this office maintenance man who lives in Westchester and who spends all his time working in the managing director's stately country house? And which new business prospect necessitated a three-week trip to the Caribbean?

This rich cake, which used to be divided up between the board and the senior executives without reference to busybodies from outside the agency, now has to be stripped of its icing. Lean and prudent management is the new order of the day, and those generous annual shareouts will soon have to include investors, some of whom might not take kindly to the more exotic items that figure as expenses in the balance sheet. It's a painful process, this full disclosure.

Finally, there are some adjustments to be made in the way the agency reports its own successes. Wall Street is actually going to take these announcements seriously, and the natural optimism of the press release, which rounds out figures to the nearest million or two, might backfire when income falls below stated expectations. Restraint and accuracy, which are not always evident in agency self-promotion, will have to replace airy and overhopeful hype.

It is even possible that there might be moments during the long months of preparation when the agency principals have second thoughts about going public. The obligations and restrictions mount up, and a future of behaving in a responsible and businesslike manner lies ahead, sacrifices that would be intolerable were it not for the fat checks that have mentally already been put in the bank, and the gratifying prospect of commercial respectability, one's name in the stock-market listings, equal status with the tycoons. The ego will at last be fed. And, one fine day, it is. The public offering is made.

The weeks immediately following are happy weeks for our three young men. Their bank managers give them lunch and talk about portfolio management. Their staff, who have calculated the size of their winnings, look at them with a satisfying mixture of envy and admiration. Every morning, they turn to the share listings and see themselves immortalized, rich, and successful. And during the tedium of the daily round of meetings, they can divert themselves by planning how they are going to spend their money.

Bigger and more impressive houses are usually top of the list, and particulars from smart real estate agents start to outnumber marketing documents and conference reports in the attaché case. And then there is the choice of a suitably expensive hobby: for some the purchase of a speedboat; for others, art or opera or vintage cars or first-growth clarets. Maybe a condo in Florida, as well. Why not? We can afford it.

In many cases, the money goes out as suddenly as it came in. And at the same time, the days and years of reckoning begin, which can be rather depressing if that first flush of extravagance has taken care of most of the liquid cash. Future wealth depends on the agency's performance and the value of its shares, and this is pointed out with irritating regularity by the swarm of security analysts that invades the agency every month.

For the most part, these walking computers know little about advertising and probably care less. They're interested in figures—bigger figures. Every quarter, every six months, every year. How are they going to react to the news that you have resigned an account because the client is congenitally incapable of recognizing a good campaign when it's stuck under his nose? They will not be pleased. They will suck their teeth and shake their heads. Temperamental behavior, they will say to themselves. It will revive their suspicions that advertising, for all its businesslike veneer, is still erratic and unprofessional, subject to whim and fancy instead of hardheaded management disciplines.

So the share price will drop—and with it, the paper fortunes of the agency principals.

The pressure to produce bigger profits and better dividends will have an increasing effect on the way in which the agency does business. When growth is an absolute requirement, the search for new clients will become more frenzied and, in some cases, much less discriminating. Accounts that the agency wouldn't previously have touched for one reason or another—perhaps because the client is known to be a bullying megalomaniac or a notoriously late payer—now become acceptable, even desirable. Who cares if the man is a foaming idiot with a taste for kicking account executives around? Nobody said that life as a publicly quoted company would be easy, and his account will provide the extra billings needed to toss to the security analysts.

It will keep them quiet for a month or two and then, as relentless as slugs after lettuce, they'll be wanting more. But where is it going to come from? It's all very well being one of the fastest-growing and most promising agencies around, but that's a position with limited prospects. An agency can't keep growing indefinitely on purely domestic business, and if it doesn't keep growing, those security analysts will be dispensing gloom and talking down the share price. The daily dips into the *Wall Street Journal*'s listings won't be quite so pleasant. Instead of the warm glow, there will be a twinge of disappointment as the shares falter, then slump. Relative poverty! What can be done?

Some time ago, the Saatchi brothers started to promote a one-word solution to their growth problem, and it has been more successful (for them, at least) than the

93

"unique selling proposition" in its finest hour ever was for Ted Bates (now a member of the Saatchi collection). That one word—as yet unrecognized by the *Oxford English Dictionary* but doubtless soon to get in there—was *globalization*.

Like *understains* and *empathy,* two other contributions that advertising has made to the English language, *globalization* was a new label for something that already existed. For many years before the word was coined, the large American agencies had been globalizing all over the place. It used to be called servicing international clients. Thus, if an agency had Colgate or Procter & Gamble business in the United States, it was natural to extend the arrangement into those more primitive markets such as Europe. Client and agency understood each other, they were used to working together, and they could transplant doctrines and working methods developed in Cincinnati to less enlightened parts of the world.

In those days, it was strictly an American preserve, because only the United States had the giant clients—Coca-Cola, IBM, Ford, Procter, Colgate—whose foreign budgets were big enough to justify an agency branch office. These branch offices rumbled along, picking up local business where they could, securely based on the income provided by the mother client across the Atlantic. British agencies found it very frustrating; they could pitch until they were hoarse for the British slice of an American giant, only to run up against the impregnable client/agency relationship that was so carefully maintained at Head Office, USA.

The great achievement of the Saatchis was to leapfrog all the long and usually fruitless nonsense of pitching for big American clients and just buy the agencies that had the business they wanted, using paper provided by the City. Once they had shown that this could be done, not just in the

United States but all over the world, there was obviously a need to find a brave new description for it, and for the more wide-ranging marketing opportunities that could make it attractive to clients. We can imagine the search for the perfect label, the various combinations of international, multinational, growth, progress, wider business horizons, and a dozen other words and phrases that partly explained but never encapsulated the girdling of the earth.

None of them was quite right. None of them had corporate sex appeal. None of them was *new*. And then, enshrined in the pages of the *Harvard Business Review*, Maurice Saatchi found the magic word, credit (or blame) for which should go to Professor Theodore Levitt: globalization!

Well, the good professor may have invented it, but the Saatchis and the advertising business have now taken it over and sold it. Apart from its brevity and its world-conquering associations of thinking big, globalization fits the bill so neatly because it is not just the agency beating its chest; the client can join in, as well. We can all globalize together, treating the world as one market, leaping national boundaries with our toothpaste and soft drinks and detergent, selling aspirin and acne remedies from Nome to Tierra del Fuego, to thousands of millions of consumers who are going to be thrilled to find their favorite brand of catsup in every corner of the earth. Who could resist? It is marketing's Promised Land.

Access to the Promised Land, unfortunately, is only available to agencies and clients who are not only globally aware but globally capable, and it is here that the British agency—publicly quoted and successful though it may be— is weak. Giant clients can't be expected to globalize with domestic agencies. And sooner or later, without those giant clients, the growth rate will slow down, the security analysts will resume their nagging, and the agency may well be seized and swallowed in a takeover. In the end, there's nothing to do but go over to the home of the biggest, most globalized clients and seek an arrangement with one of the mammoths of Madison Avenue. (Although nowadays they are likely to have less glamorous addresses like Third Avenue or Sixth or that distant netherworld called downtown. But what the hell; it's only a long cab ride from the Pierre or the Carlyle.)

America the Bountiful

Gadgets are popular with advertising people, particularly if they are highly priced and supersonic, and so the suitable way for a British adman, as I once was, to begin any reconnaissance trip to the conglomerates in New York is by Concorde. It may be cramped, but in a way that adds to the delightful feeling that we are members of a small and exclusive club, traveling with people who are as busy and important as we are. Why, we might easily find ourselves rubbing knees with a famous film director or David Frost or some Texan squillionaire who has forgotten where he's left his private jet. As the passengers file on board, they size each other up—not in an obvious way, of course—to reassure themselves that they are among fellow movers and shakers. Frivolous holidaymakers who are starting to punish the free champagne at ten in the morning are ignored because they have no place here. Concorde is not for them; it is for the lords of the stratosphere, the executives for whom time is money. The plane takes off to the sound of a fusillade of clicks as attaché cases are snapped open, and documents are shuffled assiduously all the way across the Atlantic. A working day in the mecca of advertising lies ahead.

It takes several visits for any European emissary to adjust to the monumental opulence of the world of the big New York agencies—the acres of oiled teak and leather and plate glass, the vertiginous views from the power offices (always on the corner of the building, so that the visitor has a choice of vertigo), the vastness of the budgets and salaries, the length of the limousines, the size of the lobsters at the Palm Restaurant, as big as basking sharks, the price of burgundy at the Four Seasons—it's all so wonderfully excessive. In fact, it's advertising heaven. Until you look at the advertising that pays for it.

Twenty-five years ago, the best American advertising was the best in the world, and British visitors used to return from New York with tales of commercials that might have been written by Woody Allen; commercials with extraordinary people—black, Jewish, Italian, all incredibly *ethnic*—saying funny things in those funny accents of theirs, minor comic masterpieces. And the same approach could be seen in print advertising. Instead of demented housewives comparing soiled clothing or the endless repetition of leaden slogans, one or two brave souls were producing witty, colloquial advertisements that assumed the general public had a sense of humor.

Bill Bernbach was selling ugly, unpretentious little cars by being honest and amusing about what a Volkswagen could and couldn't do, and making the obscure Levy's Jewish bakery famous with one small poster campaign. David Ogilvy was selling Hathaway shirts and Rolls-Royces with intelligent copy that contained words of more than two syllables. And, wonder of wonders, it seemed to be effective as well as noticeable. The agencies that were doing what was then called "creative advertising" flourished.

The larger, older agencies who weren't doing creative advertising had a comforting line of argument if anyone should suggest that their work might benefit from a little humor or originality. It's all very well, they would say, for these rinky-dink advertisers with tiny budgets. They can afford to make jokes and take risks (conveniently forgetting the risk and the waste involved in running advertising that is either not noticed or actively disliked). But we, the big agencies, are dealing with vast budgets and important products—cornflakes and detergents and laxatives—and we're not talking to a handful of East Coast intellectuals. We're talking to Middle America, and they won't buy that kind of cute shit.

But at that time, quite a few large clients weren't so sure. Why shouldn't a housewife in Kansas have a sense of humor? Why should noticeable and effective advertising be restricted to small budgets when big budgets would make it even more noticeable and effective? Were dirty shirt collars and constipation really such grave and important issues in consumers' lives that they couldn't be treated with a lightness of touch? If the new advertising could sell cars and bread, why couldn't it sell coffee and aspirin and beer?

For a number of years, creative advertising was in danger of taking over Madison Avenue, and some old agencies felt obliged to invest in some window dressing, hiring high-profile creative directors to show that they, too, were ready to clamber on the bandwagon if it should really start

99

rolling. These hirings usually ended in tears, but it was an indication of how seriously the old agencies took the threat posed by the upstarts.

Ironically, the beginning of the end for creative advertising was probably helped along by one of the upstarts herself. Mary Wells, who had produced brilliant work for Benson & Hedges 100s and Braniff Airlines, responded to a recession in the American economy by saying that times were getting harder and that selling should get harder, too. No more jokes, boys. Let's get the presenter out of retirement and put him back on camera, holding the product and selling for all he's worth.

The sigh of relief from the traditional agencies must have been audible all over midtown Manhattan as the flash in the pan flickered, then petered out. It had been an anxious few years.

Today, the old heroes have either disappeared or grown too tired and rich to bother anymore, and American advertising, for the most part, is in the hands of committees instead of individuals. They have succeeded in bringing back the days when you could look through a magazine or watch an hour or two of television without once being disturbed by a hint of originality. The commercials are once again dull and predictable, and many old stereotypes have popped out of the woodwork: the clean-cut young people capering around to the accompaniment of jingles, the lantern-jawed men driving cars across deserts or drinking beer, the desperately sincere presenters, the women pouting at the camera, the adorable families going into ecstasies over Mom's meat loaf—they're all back, coining their residuals, tricked out in modern clothes and modern haircuts but otherwise firmly rooted in the past. To complete the evening's entertainment, there are those wash-day widows from Cincinnati, Mrs. Procter and Mrs. Gamble, comparing their grubby garments. But they're in a special category, since they never really went away; like death and taxes, they are always with us.

There is no great relief to be had from turning off the TV and picking up a magazine. Even *The New Yorker,* which was once the setting for some of the most memorable and influential print advertising ever produced, from Volkswagen and Polaroid to Hathaway and Avis, is now stuffed with ponderous plugs for businessmen's hotels and a bewildering variety of running shoes.

The decline in American advertising should be taken as a warning by British agencies, because what happens in New York tends to happen, some years later, in London. But for the moment, the visiting British executive finds, perhaps to his surprise, that what he has said so often might actually be true: British advertising is now the best in the world.

And so it is with a pleasant but well-concealed feeling of creative superiority that he steps out of the elevator on the thirty-eighth floor and into the conglomerate's den. More teak and glass and cunning lighting, and the ruffle of air conditioning. Or is it someone counting money?

He is led into the corner office to meet—or since he's in New York, to "meet with"—one of the conglomerate's top men. This is an exploratory visit, so there's nothing as formal as a meeting with the executive committee or the board—just two guys talking over philosophies and possibilities, followed by a two-hundred-dollar lunch.

The top man's office, it has to be said, is damned impressive. For a start, there are those dizzy double views, with the worker ants barely visible thirty-eight floors below as they scurry along the street. No two-hundred-dollar lunch for them; probably some kind of low-rent sandwich in a brown paper bag.

Inside, the view is wealthy. Graphic starkness and architectural minimalism might be appropriate in Covent Garden, but not here. There is an abundance of carpet, suede, rosewood, polished granite, brushed steel—but not a vulgar abundance. It is extremely tastefully done. Mies van der Rohe would have approved. In fact, it's the kind of office that can give you second thoughts about graphic starkness, which seems a little bleak and uncomfortable by comparison. There is one touch of minimalism: The spotless, gleaming desk is bare except for a leather document folder and a few hundred dollars' worth of Mont Blanc pens and pencils. And behind the desk, barbered and manicured and shoe-shined to perfection, glowing with a tan acquired in the Hamptons (summer) or the Caribbean (winter), is the man himself.

He is damned impressive, too: a heavy hitter in a silk suit, with those impossibly perfect American teeth much in evidence as he smiles and chats in a relaxed arm-around-the-shoulder style that makes you feel like an old and intimate friend. Right away, he confesses to being a great admirer of British advertising in general and the work being done by your agency in particular. And he's done his homework. He knows the accounts and the campaigns, the billings and the share price. He sympathizes with the difficulties of achieving better figures and bigger dividends. He has the same cross to bear; his shareholders are always kicking his ass, too. It's a hell of a way to earn a living.

But, as you discover in the course of the next few days, it's a hell of a living, what with the duplex, the summer place in the Hamptons, the forty-five-foot boat, the condominium in Vail, and those minor odds and ends—constant limos and accounts in a dozen good restaurants—that make living in New York more than tolerable. And, as the chats continue, you discover something else: The man is not just a professional charmer. He knows about art and music and books and wine. He knows Europe better than you do. He has a healthy sense of humor. What a pleasure it would be to work with him. And yet . . . how can you reconcile this cultured and discriminating fellow with some of the crap turned out by his agency?

The contrast between the highly articulate and intelligent individuals who work in American advertising and the banal junk they often produce is a puzzle that is perhaps partly solved by looking at some figures.

There are at least fifty U.S. corporations whose advertising budgets exceed $200 million worldwide. A $200 million account delivers $30 million income to the agency. For this kind of money, the client expects and demands advertising that he considers to be effective, but advertising effectiveness is extraordinarily difficult to measure with any kind of accuracy. After all the research and testing has been done, there is still room for debate and opinion. The client's opinion may, and frequently does, differ from the way the agency sees things. If persuasion fails, the agency can either agree with the client or kiss $30 million good-bye, and it's easy enough to guess what will happen. Business is business, and if there are some small qualms about expediency and compromise, these can always be soothed in one way or another. *Living well is the best revenge.*

This may sound simplistic and unkind, but what other answer is there? Could any sane adult reveal with a straight face that he was sincerely involved in the Doublemint Gum commercials, the painkiller sagas, the dramas of the postnasal drip and germ-infested bathrooms and

103

greasy T-shirts that take up ten percent or more of American TV viewing time? Nobody could devote a career to this with any enthusiasm were it not for the money.

That in itself is no crime, and there are plenty of honest and cheerfully cynical people in advertising who will privately admit to turning out puerile work for the rewards it brings in. For the others, there are different ways of coming to terms with the problem, and the higher they proceed up the corporate ladder, the easier it is to distance themselves from creative matters. Finally, although advertising is the product their corporations sell, they themselves cease to be advertising men and become instead international businessmen. And the liaisons they arrange with other international businessmen have very little to do with creative philosophies other than the creation of a few more million.

It's something to think about on the flight back to London. Like it or not, that's the way the big league is, and if your agency has been invited to join, there are a number of reasons for accepting the invitation.

Greed

While this is not something to be aired over the conference table with the rest of the board, it is impossible to resist making a few rosy calculations about the extent of personal gain that would accrue as a result of joining a conglomerate. The couple of million that came in when the agency went public now looks modest when put against the many millions that have been hinted at in the event of a successful international deal.

Boredom

After a few years of running an agency, a certain repetition creeps into the mechanics of management. The same old problems reappear with new faces attached to them—disgruntled staff, disenchanted clients—and what was once a stimulating challenge turns into familiar drudgery. As a top-level man in an international conglomerate, however, much of this day-to-day tedium can be delegated. Who can forget the international executive creative director, for example, who spent his time touring the offices of the world in his lofty capacity as corporate critic? Pausing in each office just long enough to dispense a few days' worth of wisdom, he was well out of the firing line by the time his suggestions had been implemented. If they proved to be disastrous, he would complain on his next visit that they had been misinterpreted. Try again, he'd say. I have a plane to catch.

Opportunities such as this exist in many walks of top conglomerate life, and for a few years, providing a person can endure endless first-class hotels and travel, it makes a change from the continuing grind of dealing with the politics and administration of a single office, although it does play havoc with the digestion.

Self-Defense

More and more, any agency that doesn't belong to an international network will find itself excluded from international clients. As the blessings of globalization spread, so clients will appoint a single chain of agencies that can service them wherever they happen to be. Having a sound local client list is no lasting protection, because it's always possible that some clients themselves may be taken over and extracted from the agency to fit in with some grand global plan. One or two bad breaks like this and the agency will be in trouble, wide open to a bargain-basement takeover offer.

A Sense of Mission

The optimist's theory, which permits the cash to be taken without the stigma of selling out, goes something like this:

> We know that the advertising produced by our prospective purchasers is wretched stuff compared with our own memorable and original campaigns, but we have been assured that we shall be creatively independent, left alone to do our noble work without interference from our owners. In fact, they admire our advertising; they've said so time and again. Why buy us if they're going to change us? But that alone, as comforting as it may be, is not the end of it. The optimist's mission is not merely to maintain his high creative standards, but to impose them on the rest of the conglomerate's world. Global excellence, and stinking rich to boot!

106

It's a heady and worthwhile ambition. Agency networks have been talking about it for many years. Some have tried, and some are trying. None has so far succeeded in burying the demented housewives and the other grotesque characters who appear on television every night to mug us in the living room, though there's always hope.

Any one of the reasons listed above might be enough to convince the most stoutly independent of agencies that big is beautiful, and when added together they have proved irresistible. There are today more than twenty agency conglomerates whose billings total a billion dollars or more, and there are no obvious signs that this passion for size will lessen over the next ten or twenty years. It keeps the shareholders and the agency principals happy. It keeps the clients happy. It keeps Concorde more or less full. Voltaire had the right idea: "All is for the best in the best of all possible worlds." He should have been in advertising.

Tribal
Customs

Sociologists have always been fascinated by the habits and behavior of small groups who create worlds of their own that are, to a greater or lesser extent, detached from what the rest of us call real life. From the lost tribes of the Amazon basin to the members of the New York Yacht Club or the Royal Yacht Squadron, it is possible to see how these groups attempt to structure a private environment, complete with its own private rules and rewards, inaccessible to outsiders.

Advertising is just another example, although so far it seems to have escaped the attention of the learned gentlemen who publish studies on behavioral oddities. They're missing a treat. Not since the court of Louis XIV has there been such a ripe blend of intrigue, self-promotion, and rampant consumption, the more conspicuous the better.

This is not confined to any particular nationality, and the traveling advertising executive will find kindred spirits in New York, London, Paris, Düsseldorf, or Melbourne. The languages and accents may change, but the aspirations and expense accounts will be every bit as grandiose as they are back home. Unlike the Amazon tribes, this is an international group, and it is motivated by an international urge. The pursuit of status, in all its delightful variations, is advertising's favorite game.

In broad terms, it can be divided into visible affluence or recognized professional excellence (which, as we shall see later, is a preserve dominated by the creative side of the business). In a way, it is a touching example of an industry's belief in what it does—the high priests of promotion and consumption practicing what they preach and loving every minute of it. Since so much time and effort is expended during the working day on selling the benefits of novelty (the word *new* being used whenever you can get away with it), it is not surprising that advertising people are suckers for the status conferred by new toys. In the distant days when cordless telephones were in their primitive evolutionary stage and were not generally available, it was an odds-on bet that the man in the restaurant making ostentatious phone calls from the comfort of his table was an advertising man. The apparatus might then have been a cumbersome box with a whip antenna, and not soupproof if a waiter should trip over it, but nevertheless . . . *nobody else had one,* and it marked him as a man apart. (It was also an agency chairman who pioneered the refinement of installing two phones in the car so that the chauffeur could tell all incoming callers that his lordship was on the other line.)

The mobile telephone is, or was, a perfect example of achieving status by gadgets, because other people couldn't help being aware of it, and if you have ever had the disagreeable experience of sitting next to an advertising man "giving phone" in an otherwise-pleasant restaurant, you will undoubtedly remember the occasion. But after all, what is the point of having a private, unseen gadget? As someone unkindly remarked about those self-congratulatory corporate advertising campaigns, it's like urinating down your leg in the middle of a dark forest at midnight. You might get a warm feeling out of it, but nobody else notices.

Almost as perfect an accessory, and certainly less noisy, is the Filofax, which has become so much a physical appendage that babies born to advertising parents will shortly start to enter the world clutching them in their chubby fists. The Filofax has a lot going for it: Too big for a pocket, too fat for many handbags, and too small to justify an attaché case, it needs to be carried in full view. It can very easily be made to bulge, and while the owner may know that the bulge is largely made up of unpaid bills, the outside world can be led to believe that it is made up of privileged information: the personal numbers of captains of industry, the details of hectic international commitments, Mick Jagger's address in the Loire, and all kinds of other elitist jottings that are hinted at but never disclosed.

A popular addition to the bulge is the wad of airline tickets protruding from the back so that we know the owner is just about to go somewhere exotic or important. And the final obligatory touch is that the cover should look scuffed and well-traveled. Only amateurs and junior brand managers would dream of displaying anything as gauche as a stiff new Filofax. The single permissible exception to this is the millionaire's model, with a cover made from crushed baby ostrich or the soft underbelly of a peccary, priced at a thousand dollars and up and explained away with mock embarrassment as the gift of a grateful client. (Actually, it went down on expenses as office supplies.)

But these are merely fringe items, marginal trifles that have lost most of their cachet now that they have been devalued by wider and cheaper availability. When your office messenger has a bulging Filofax and your hairdresser has a cordless phone, it is time to move on—and up.

Cars, of course, are to the advertising business what jewels are to the professional courtesan: public and instantly recognizable signals of success. More often than not, the cars preferred by the rising executive are unsuitable or inconvenient, or both. To the uninformed, it might appear curious that a man who lives and works in the middle of the city needs a four-wheel-drive Range Rover or a 160 mph Porsche Carrera to negotiate five or six miles of congested streets every day, but that's exactly the point. The last thing one wants to be seen driving is a practical car. Sales reps drive practical cars.

In every garage, therefore, you will see a continually changing (it wouldn't do to have last year's model) selection of specialized and extravagantly priced transport, designed for either the muddy fields of Connecticut or the expressway. But should you be indelicate enough to ask the drivers of these machines why all this horsepower is necessary when most of the city is a vast, barely moving traffic jam, they will have the answer ready: It's for the weekends, to get out to the country.

A restless longing, something not unlike spring fever, attacks many advertising executives as soon as they have achieved sufficient wealth or creditworthiness to see beyond their mortgage. There is a yearning for simple bucolic pleasures, a need to return to the damp green bosom of the countryside, where the Porsche is seldom seen and the mournful hoot of the client is never heard. And so, months of weekends are devoted to the investigation of country houses, farms, deconsecrated Baptist chapels, barns, and picturesque pigsties until the perfect little retreat is discovered and snapped up. Back to basics! God's clean air, bird song at dusk, and not an Italian restaurant within fifty miles.

Naturally, it is not enough simply to own a country property; other people must know about it, and one of the most satisfactory ways of telling them is through the medium of rustic accoutrements.

For two days a week, providing there are no serious meetings, it is possible to arrive at the office dressed in outfits that smack of a horse show in Bedford. On Fridays (going out) and on Mondays (just come in), there is an excuse to put aside city clothes and come to work reeking of farmyard chic—the Ralph Lauren swineherd's jacket, the Paul Smith corduroy trousers with genuine bone fly buttons, oiled Guernsey sweaters, moleskin jackets, hunting boots, tweed hats, mud-stained Barbours—anything that declares the wearer to be the owner of something more than a small co-op on the Upper East Side.

And it goes on from there. Midweek deliveries to the office of rough country wines, subscriptions (free, thanks to the Media Department) to *Town & Country,* prolonged telephone conversations, preferably overheard by other members of the agency, with Smith & Hawken and tree surgeons, meetings with red-faced men in tweeds who breed retrievers, and always, somewhere on prominent but casual display in the office, one or two objects that hint at rural pursuits.

A brace of freshly shot birds is ideal except for the rather limited shelf life, but shooting sticks, binoculars, boxes of twelve-bore ammunition, and sailing paraphernalia are acceptable alternatives.

As for the country house itself, more or less the same rules apply as for cars: Appearance is everything, and to hell with the cost and inconvenience. Consequently, the traditional country house is not given any serious consideration, being too small and manageable and normal. If true grandeur, such as an estate with its own park, is temporarily out of financial reach, the chosen property should be in some way extraordinary—a Gothic folly, a disused nunnery, a derelict brewery—and it should have enormous rooms. There is, after all, the full-size pool table to accommodate, as well as the half-acre Edwardian kitchen discovered in an architectural salvage depot. The rolling vista, indoors as well as outside, is essential. Anything less would fail to impress the fortunate few who will be invited for bracing weekends in front of a roaring television set watching football.

Such is the pressure of advertising life that escaping to the country for the weekend is not enough. It was probably a mistake to put a fax machine in the mudroom, and office problems are not sufficiently far away to permit the recharging of the batteries that is such a vital part of the executive's busy year. What he needs is time to unwind, a chance to step away from it all, to read—God, there's never a *moment* to read—to contemplate broader horizons, to refresh the intellect a million miles from the gossip and intrigue of the business. And so he goes on vacation, frequently with other advertising people.

They may not actually travel together, but they will usually choose a destination where there is a high possibility of bumping into one another. The reason for this is partly to avoid boredom but mainly to protect themselves from the horrors of anonymity. To be alone, unrecognized and unimportant among a bunch of foreign savages would be a severe setback to ego and status. A group, however, can create its own cocoon. The insiders' club can continue to function, independent of the natives or the local environment.

There are several parts of the world where, depending on the time of the year, groups of brightly colored advertising people can be found nesting in bars and restaurants overlooking beaches and ski slopes. And there is one favored spot that can be guaranteed to offer the observer a whiff of the essence of it all, a sometimes uncomfortably close view of the advertising man at play.

St. Paul de Vence lies in the foothills of the Alps Maritimes, half an hour or so from Nice airport. The village is small and was once charming. It has now given itself up to the tourist industry, and the narrow streets are lined with shops selling *folklorique* souvenirs, every conceivable type of Kodak film, and clumsy artifacts made from olive wood. Buses full of cameras with people attached arrive at regular intervals throughout the season, and the old men who play *pétanque* in the little square outside the café have had their pictures taken so many times that they fall quite naturally into photogenic poses. An evil-tempered policeman is on duty to repel motorists, and it is not uncommon to see a dozen or more cars trying to reverse in unison as he sends them out the way they came in. One way and another, you might think, St. Paul is not quite the haven of calm a weary executive longs for after the bruising encounters of agency life.

But in the midst of this seething mass of cars and trippers is a refuge—equally seething, to be sure, but seething in the right way, with the right kind of people. The Colombe d'Or hotel, which used to provide food and shelter for artists like Picasso and writers (James Baldwin was for many years an almost permanent fixture at the bar), now caters to the luminaries of the advertising business: directors of commercials, TV network bosses, top agency executives, photographers, the higher-paid writers and art directors and the occasional personal assistant, usually a young lady whose sunglasses are bigger than her swimsuit.

What draws them here, apart from the obvious lure of seeing one another, is that the layout of the Colombe d'Or might have been expressly designed to accommodate a group of people who want to be seen to be privileged. It is the perfect enclave, prominent and yet sealed off from the common crowd by a high stone wall and sufficiently small in scale for intimacy with other guests to be unavoidable. Privacy is not easy to come by at the Colombe d'Or, but then privacy is not what the guests are looking for.

The hotel is, however, extremely pretty, with a large terrace overlooking a long and spectacular view. And it is on the terrace under the bleached canvas umbrellas that the refugees from the advertising world take their ease over a protracted Sunday lunch.

But first, an apéritif. As the bar fills up, cries of delight fill the warm, scented air: "David! Sally! Tony! Jane! What are *you* doing here? Managed to ditch the client? What a nice surprise!" The real surprise, of course, would be to enter the bar and not see a familiar face, but luckily there's no chance of that on a fine Sunday in July.

The bartender, a man of scrupulous surliness, mixes endless *kirs royales* as the gossip mingles with the cigar smoke. Old Barry has been spotted having a clandestine dinner with his hot-lipped secretary in Mougins. Louise and

Adrian were overheard having a flaming row in their room last night, and they haven't appeared since. Terry—what a brat!—left his filthy sneakers outside the bedroom door to be cleaned and the chambermaid threw them away. Serves him right. And, as the *kirs royales* go down and the noise level goes up, plans for lunch are compared. You're eating here? Terrific. So are we. The food's not great, but it's that view that matters, isn't it? Why don't we share a table?

They drift out in groups of four or six or more, baying for *blanc de blancs* and ice buckets, and settle themselves around the terrace, Ray·Ban sunglasses glittering, panama hats cocked rakishly over one eye, clothing fashionably rumpled. This is the life! Here we are, among our own kind, getting away from it all.

Before any consideration can be given to the food, there are a few obligatory minutes of table-hopping, cheek-kissing, and backslapping as contact is made with anyone who was missed at the bar, and loud arrangements are proposed for dinner. The other people eating lunch, civilians judging by their clothes and their curious interest in the menu, look slightly bemused. They assumed they had come to France, but instead find themselves in deepest London.

The waiters are used to the antics of their Sunday customers, and often visibly bored by them. Unlike the Italians, who are temperamentally equipped to treat lunch as a circus, the French take the business of eating more seriously, and they disapprove when food is picked at, dusted with a fine coating of cigarette ash, and then pushed aside. But they keep the wine coming and console themselves with the thought that the season can't last forever.

Neither can lunch. Indeed, he who lingers too long over the coffee and marc risks arriving at the hotel pool too late to find a parking spot. Anyone who is familiar with

France will know the tall glass boxes that are placed out in the street with dripping rows of slowly revolving chickens on display to tempt the passerby. Take away the glass box and substitute human bodies for chickens, and there you have the Colombe d'Or pool on a Sunday afternoon. It is not big. One overweight TV producer jumping in the deep end can spray half the sunbathers who are packed, oily haunch to oily haunch, along the flagstones surrounding the water. But this lack of space, which some might find claustrophobic, has a social plus: You can continue your lunchtime conversation with your friends even though they're on the other side of the pool. You have to shout a bit to make yourself heard, but that's all part of the fun.

Eventually, as the shadows lengthen, the sunbathers drift off to prepare themselves for the rigors of an evening on the Côte d'Azur, and the process can begin all over again. Knots of revelers wait in the bar or on the terrace for taxis to arrive and lost cars to be found, and the attractions of various restaurants are discussed. Food is of minor importance; ambience is all. Is it the kind of place people like us should be seen in? The groups roar off, taking their ambience with them, and the only couples who dine alone are either having problems or having an affair.

Perhaps the only thing lacking in an otherwise-ideal world—the only thing one misses, really—is that the office entourage can't come on vacation as well. There are too many of them, because as the advertising man leaps up the ladder of success, he collects around him a team of retainers, and the size and composition of this team is a measure of his importance in advertising society.

The ultimate aim is to be able to say, in a jocular and self-deprecating way, how completely useless one is at dealing with the mundane details of daily life. The pinnacle of uselessness can be achieved, of course, only if there is a small army at beck and call, a human infrastructure to service our hero as he deals with matters of corporate state.

There must be at least two secretaries, and between them they should administer and to a certain extent control every waking minute of their boss's life—not just his business appointments but his personal responsibilities, from making sure he pays the school bills to reminding him of his mistress's birthday. He should not be expected to remember anything, so that he can fully enjoy the role of the absent-minded dynamo. "Where am I next week? Oh God, New York." His feigned ignorance of his own movements is useful protection against questions he may not wish to answer and appointments he may not wish to keep. After a while, his staff realizes that it's a waste of time talking to him without consulting one of his ladies-in-waiting first, very much like the system employed by royalty.

There might, in addition, be a personal assistant, but not the nubile little hussy with the big sunglasses; she is temporary vacation staff. The permanent PA is more likely to be a young man in a dark suit who shadows the great man everywhere. His functions are to take notes, to pay restaurant bills, to carry documents and attaché cases, and to liaise with the secretarial unit so that he can act as a mobile memory during any time spent out of the office. He is also sent off into the rain to summon the chauffeur.

In London, agency chauffeurs are as acutely status-conscious as their employers and take great pride in having the longest, blackest, most shiny Mercedes of any member of the chauffeurs' club. (The Rolls, for some reason, is not so popular nowadays, although one agency chairman's chauffeur, a magnificently stately creature, has his own Rolls, which he drives when he's off duty.) The top chauf-

118

feurs have a fiercely competitive streak that shows itself every time they attend a function in central London, and the competition is to see who can get pole position right outside the hotel entrance at the end of the evening. Park Lane becomes a death trap of swooping limousines, and the winner is the chauffeur whose boss has to walk the shortest distance. The prize—wonderful moment!—is when the boss turns to one of his peers and offers him a lift to *his* car, which is stuck ignominiously at the end of the line.

This nucleus of four (secretaries, PA, and chauffeur) is often augmented by a personal chef. Strictly speaking, he is retained to cook nourishing and inexpensive meals for the directors' dining room, but with very little persuasion he will be happy to prepare rather more elaborate menus for private dinner parties at his employer's house.

Domestic staff are essential, but not as satisfying, since there is a limit to the number of people who can see them. It is a problem that one monumentally pretentious advertising man overcame by arranging meetings at his home on Saturday mornings. In the course of these meetings, he would excuse himself to go to the back door, often, as legend had it, dressed for the occasion in a velvet smoking jacket. Lined up outside the back door would be the servants, waiting for their wages. After a suitable period of forelock tugging and distribution of largess, the meeting would be resumed.

The retinue can stretch down to the country and even overseas, but the city is where it counts because London is where it can be seen.

The same principle of high visibility dictates the choice of sporting interests. Very few advertising men, if any, enjoy the solitary pleasures of walking or fishing. The outfits aren't glamorous enough, and the social opportunities non-existent. Shooting, skiing, golf, football (in the capacity of nonplaying patron), and sailing all have their share of supporters, but the one sport that might almost have been invented for the amusement and benefit of the advertising business is tennis.

It has just about everything. The equipment, even down to the Boris Becker Grand Slam autographed socks, is hideously expensive, and it is clearly marked with famous names and logos to show that it's expensive. There is the chance to increase the number of personal retainers by hiring Doctor Topspin, the Czechoslovakian coach. The private tennis clubs are suitably exclusive and sure to impress clients. And the social opportunities are infinite; better still, they're deductible. The most elusive of new business prospects will always come to heel when a ticket to Centre Court at Wimbledon is waved under his nose, and an overpriced bowl of strawberries and cream will often do the trick where lunch at the Ritz has failed. Game, set, and account to the agency.

We come now to the second and more specialized form of status hunting, which is practiced in a separate world of its own within the larger world of advertising. Only creative people can take part (although, given a little thought and ingenuity, no doubt something could be arranged for media planners and professors of research), and they do so with relentless enthusiasm and considerable political cunning. It is the pursuit of awards.

There are dozens—no, hundreds—to pursue. A small self-congratulatory industry has grown up over the years to celebrate the achievements of art directors, designers, writers, photographers, illustrators, TV directors, and anyone else who can claim to have had a hand in the creative process. There are awards for cinema commercials and direct-mail shots, for packaging and stationery and radio spots, for the Best Use of this and the Best Use of that: a glorious, endless torrent of certificates (suitable for framing), medals, statuettes, Plexiglas icons, silver arrows, golden pencils, and desk jewelry of all shapes and sizes. Recognition—visible, tangible, stick-it-on-the-wall recognition—is there in abundance, and it is greatly revered.

There are organizations in all major advertising cities that arrange, once a year, the collection of outstanding work and its assessment by eminent figures in the business. But since London, according to London agency people, currently produces the best advertising, it seems appropriate to see how excellence is rewarded there.

Several generous bodies have instituted awards schemes as British advertising has become a more intrusive and prosperous part of industry, and their prizes are always welcome. One institution, however, that has managed to totter along for more than twenty-five years on the brink of bankruptcy, riddled by politics and guilty of sponsoring the year's most inedible dinner, is undoubtedly the front-runner. Despite infighting, incompetence, and indigestion, the Designers and Art Directors Association (or DADA, as it is known to its intimates) is the single-most-influential source of creative fame. This is how it works.

During the post-Christmas doldrums, when there is not normally a great deal going on in most agencies apart from hangovers and skiing vacations, the creative department is uncharacteristically busy. It is reviewing all the work it has produced in the previous twelve months and selecting the campaigns and individual advertisements that it feels worthy of DADA's recognition. Naturally, all the writers and art directors consider that their personal output is vastly superior to that of their colleagues. They want to enter everything they've done, from the two-minute commercials down to the witty invitation they knocked out for the office party.

Unfortunately, DADA's entry fees are substantial. All items entered must be accompanied by a check, and so the creative director finds himself with a dilemma. If he humors his writers and art directors and submits the lot, the agency may have to lay out a few thousand pounds (real money, since it can't be claimed back from the client). The financial director will not be pleased. He already thinks the creative people cost too much, anyway. On the other hand, if the creative director edits the submissions down to a more modest and affordable number, his sensitive staff will be upset. There will be cries of favoritism and, if he decides to enter any of his own work, blatant self-promotion. It is a testing time for him, but we must leave him to get on with it, because decisions of even greater importance are being finalized over at DADA headquarters.

Each year, certain prominent and highly regarded figures are asked to act as judges of the work submitted in various categories. The judges are experts in their particular fields. In fact, they will probably have entered some of their own work in the category they're judging, a situation that some might say could lead to a less than disinterested eye when it comes to judging the inferior efforts of their competitors. But that's the way it is, and a battalion of eminent men and women (one year the figure nearly reached a hundred) is recruited to sift through the thousands of entries.

Their first job is to throw out the junk that's always entered by the optimistic or extravagant agencies. The items that survive will be properly commemorated. They will be displayed in the DADA Exhibition, and enshrined in *The Book*—a glossy volume produced each year with healthy sales guaranteed by the simple device of naming all the people connected with each piece of work shown. Thus, the list of credits under a single newspaper advertisement might include the names of the art director, the writer, the photographer or illustrator, the typographer, the advertising manager, the agency, and the client—most of whom will buy a copy on their expense accounts—not, of course, for reasons of vanity, but for reference.

The second task before the judges is to allocate the prizes, and since these can make reputations overnight, they are not awarded lightly. (Sometimes, in the case of a split decision or as a result of some determined sabotage by a vocal judge, they may not be awarded at all, which is not entirely in the spirit of the proceedings.)

The method of judging, both in the initial editing stage and the distribution of awards, is not too far off from the time-honored principle followed by cardinals when electing a new Pope: Any self-interest is encouraged and protected by secrecy. The organizers of DADA have done their best, and judges are not allowed to vote for their own work, but that still leaves plenty of leeway for the pat on the back or the knife in the ribs. A judge can favor the work of friends and torpedo the work of enemies, secure in the knowledge that nobody will ever know. Fellow judges may suspect that you have allowed personal fancy to interfere with your usual lucid and objective assessments, but there's no *proof.* Anyway, you say to yourself as you consign another poor wretch's pride and joy to oblivion, *everybody does it.*

When at last the jury sessions are over, the material is sent off to the printers who are producing *The Book,* and judges' lips are sealed on the subject of who has won what. Secrecy must be preserved for months (virtually impossible in advertising) until the awards are officially announced and

123

The Book is officially published to coincide with the highlight of the creative year, the Art Directors' Ball.

Curiously enough, not every hotel in London is prepared to give over its ballroom to this event, due to the volatile and often boisterous nature of the guests. But over the years one hotel, the Hilton, has shown considerable bravery, and it is only right that it should be mentioned here. The Hilton management long ago realized where the interests of its artistic clients lie, and it has catered accordingly; drink is copious and food is an also-ran. Each year there is chicken or duck in a mystery sauce. (The foul rumor that it is the *same* chicken or duck, untouched on the night and preserved in the bowels of the hotel kitchen for next year, cannot possibly be true.)

The evening begins with a table-hopping marathon. Everyone is here, and some of them haven't seen one another since lunchtime. And as they hop from table to table, they provide a fashion show of dazzling variety. There are dinner jackets and dress shirts with winged collars, bomber jackets and ripped T-shirts, six-inch heels and Azzedine Alaia skintight (no chicken for me) dresses, business suits, cowboy boots, Levi's, silk bustiers, sequins, three-day stubble, blue suede crepes, ponytails and earrings for the gentlemen and purple crew cuts for the ladies, Day-Glo glasses and matching socks, shapeless Japanese designer outfits in shades of crushed money, webbing bras, leather trousers, plastic sandals, Lurex ties. No wonder there are some fragile souls, still recovering from lunch, who have kept their sunglasses on. The whole thing is extremely creative.

There is a keen sense of expectation in the air. Tonight's the night when fifteen or twenty winners will be publicly anointed as the best in the business. Waiter! Another bucket of Soave Bolla! Wine is consumed at a furious rate as several hundred people try to break the world record for high-speed intoxication. The speeches will begin soon, and it would be a mistake to be sober when they do.

Experience has taught the speechmakers to be brief. Ever since one tycoon was howled down in the middle of his remarks, the rule has been three or four minutes at the most. The audience is not here to listen to platitudes about the changing face of British advertising. It wants awards, and if the preliminaries drag on for too long, there are likely to be a few bread rolls and catcalls flying around.

As the great moment approaches and the waiters perform their final sprint around the tables with armfuls of Rémy Martin bottles, it is possible to pick out of the crowd the people who think they might be called up to the dais and presented with a golden pencil. They are relatively sober, and you can see them measuring the distance from table to dais, checking out the route to make sure they can get up there in the shortest possible time—just in case, as has been known to happen, two people go up for the same award.

The main lights dim and the spotlight beams down on the rows of pencils and the piles of certificates. The president of DADA (a position held for one year) and the chairman of DADA (a permanent and thankless post) make their way up to the dais to the strains of some appropriately thrilling music, and the ceremony begins.

In each category, the work being honored is shown on slide or on film and the winner is summoned from the murk for those magical few seconds under the spotlight. Fortunately, the winners are not expected to make speeches, and fortunately the audience is generally good-natured and generous with its applause. There is always disappointment, but there is always the bottle of Rémy Martin at hand and the imminent prospect of some harmless diversion as soon as the pencils and certificates have been handed out.

Once this has been done, the evening moves into its dangerous period. The combination of drink, excitement, music, and some spectacularly revealing outfits plays havoc with restraint. The dance floor and the surrounding tables seethe with the joy of orgy: lurching figures, furtive embraces, bottom pinching, thigh squeezing, torn and wine-sodden garments, overturned chairs, prostrate bodies (still clutching their golden pencils), heads slumped among the bottles and decorum nowhere to be seen.

At least, that is how it used to be. Recently, due to the increased respectability of the business, the Art Directors' Ball has shown disturbing signs of sensible behavior. Now that art directors are businessmen, often with a seat on the board, it seems to have affected their capacity for enjoyment. Perhaps their chairmen have told them that it is not a good idea for the officers of public companies to be seen crawling around under tables and biting young women on the leg. Whatever the reason, the Art Directors' Ball is not what it used to be. A great shame, and another small indication that advertising is now taking itself *very, very seriously*.

The Ultimate Trip

Despite wealth, success, the acclaim of their colleagues, and a permanent reservation at Lutèce, there are some advertising men who feel that their talents have been insufficiently recognized. It's all very well to be on intimate terms with the chairman of Spandex International or Allied Biscuits, but they, in the end, are just businessmen. Outside their own environment, they are anonymous and, frankly, rather dull. There must be other, more stimulating people somewhere who would jump at the chance of working with a total communications expert, a legendary manipulator who almost single-handedly changed the face of the Condom Marketing Board. His skills should be put to greater and more public-spirited use, and where better than in the bright glare of politics?

But definitely not as a politician (long hours, low pay, miserable expenses)—no, the spot we're looking for is that of the éminence grise, the image doctor, the sage who advises nationally known men and women what to say and how to say it and not to pick their noses on television. Consultant to the nation's leaders! Now there's a worthy climax to a glittering career; in England, it can even lead to a knighthood.

Politics and advertising have a great deal in common. Both occupations have their quota of avid self-promoters who understand the refinements of the verbal nuance (or "weaseling," as it's sometimes called). Other shared characteristics include a fondness for knocking copy to discredit the competition, a passion for research surveys, a willingness to change horses in midstream if a faster and more expedient saddle offers itself, a keen appetite for meetings, and an even keener appetite for the trappings of importance. Altogether, it promises to be a rare and fruitful meeting of minds and ambitions.

The politician as client poses some interesting problems, most of which stem from the fact that in this case— very unusual in advertising—the client is also the product, and frequently the product is extremely badly packaged. The clothes look as though they've been rescued from a fire sale, there is an unfortunate jowliness around the chops (and we all know how television will add at least another five unflattering pounds), the teeth are crooked and dingy, and the hairstyle—good grief, that hairstyle!—could only have been achieved with a lawn mower and a can of acrylic spray. When looked at objectively, through the eyes of the image doctor, the raw material needs a drastic overhaul.

Objectivity needs to be exercised with some delicacy because we are treading on some thin-shelled eggs: The self-perception of politicians is rarely less than flattering, and to be told that the carefully cultivated public face is an unattractive mess might ruin the client/agency relationship before it has had a chance to get established. How simple it would be if we could just dispatch the budding President to the art department to be repackaged; unfortunately, the process has to be carried out little by little, one tactful step at a time.

It would be a virtually impossible task except for the political ambitions of the client, which are so consuming that the occasional humiliating dent to the self-esteem can be justified as the necessary means to a glorious end. This is the tie that binds, and the image doctor knows it. All he has to do is to contain his impatience and deal with the various imperfections as diplomatically as he can. Today the hair, tomorrow the teeth.

Appearance, in all its details, is perhaps the most straightforward part of marketing a politician. Good haircuts and clothes, and if necessary a little dieting and cosmetic dentistry, are not difficult to arrange. The other adjustments that need to be made, since they involve changing habits developed over many years, are more complex. They can be classified, for the sake of the strategy document, under the headings of technique and content.

129

Technique

The product thinks he is a good public speaker; more than that, he considers himself an orator, a master of the inspirational speech, capable of setting his audience alight on any subject from the threats posed to the nation's health by contaminated hamburgers to creeping development around

Tuxedo Park. Give him any burning issue and he will expound on it with barely a pause for breath, at great length.

The difficulty here is that the rhetoric, when listened to with the critical ear of the image doctor, is a matted tangle of circumlocution, hedging, and repetition, and while repetition is often desirable in advertising, the other two mannerisms certainly aren't. Brevity and clarity are what we're after, something that will fit into a thirty-second spot or onto a poster, but years of waffling can't be eradicated overnight. In any case, as the product keeps saying, the issues here are too complicated to be explained in two or three glib sentences.

Well, the rascal's going to have to learn, because we in the advertising business know how difficult it is to get one simple thought into the public skull, let alone a whole mass of qualifications and escape clauses. The habits of a political lifetime will have to be modified. Keep it clear and keep it short.

Content

1 3 0   But keep *what* clear? Of all the available topics, there are always a few favorites that can be guaranteed vote-getters if a popular point of view can be memorably expressed, if you can take it and make it your own. This is the core of the campaign—what the product stands for—and to make sure there aren't any hasty and ill-judged mistakes, it is usually necessary to send an expedition to rummage down among the grass roots and commune with that anonymous but influential consultant who is known as the man in the street.

He is regarded with mixed feelings by the advertising business because of his unpredictable nature. He has been known to miss the point of some damn clever campaigns, claiming that he doesn't know what they're talking about. He is suspected of harboring a certain mistrust of advertising, which he sometimes feels is trying to persuade him to buy something he doesn't want, and yet—according to him—he's far too wily to be influenced by it. The other mugs may fall for it but not him.

Nevertheless, he is flattered to be consulted, and once in a while he will be worth his weight in questionnaires because he will occasionally give his blessing to an advertising proposition. And when he does, the agency wheels him in as the definitive salesman. The man in the street thinks it's great! Who are we to argue with the voice of the public?

In the case of political advertising, there is also what might be called an inbuilt negative factor that must be taken into account when analyzing research: If anything, the man in the street distrusts politicians even more than he distrusts advertising. But where he can cast his vote for one or none of a dozen or more brands of margarine, his voting choice here is limited to two or three possibilities, and civic duty requires him to vote for one of them. So vote he does, with enthusiasm or indifference, in a very restricted field.

The arguments against political advertising are usually confined to discussions about the oversimplification of an enormously complicated subject—what I would do if I was running the country—and there is no doubt that advertising has helped some mediocre men and women to squeak into office because of their ability to look sincere and intelligent for a few minutes in front of the cameras. A plausible fool has a greater chance of being elected than a more worthy candidate who is not as accomplished at self-presentation. But politics have probably always been like that; modern methods just make it more apparent.

It's easy enough to see why politicians are attracted to agencies, and it's understandable that some agency people are attracted, ideologically or for the base hope of future reward, to politicians. For most of the people in the agency, however, working on a political account is something of a trial. Every day is a crisis. The work has to be done instantly, and is changed constantly in response to polls or the latest pronouncements of competitors. The client is even more of an egomaniac than the chairman of Tissues International. And there is the ticklish question of individual political beliefs. It is inconceivable that every member of the agency would vote the same way in an election; and yet, unless a separate group of volunteers is set up, some people will find themselves working for a candidate they'd rather see deported than elected.

But for the top man, the ace communicator with his vital role to play in forging the nation's destiny, it is sheer heaven. There he is, in the studio with the candidate, in the radio car with the candidate, up and down the country and in and out of Westminster or Washington with the candidate, maybe even photographed for the national press with (or three paces behind) the candidate. Peripheral fame! It was never like this with the Condom Marketing Board, and it's heady, addictive stuff.

That side of it is rarely admitted. The official reasons for taking on a politician as a client are (for the press release) a conviction that the country would be a better place if the candidate was elected and (for the board meeting) the prospect of patronage if the campaign is successful. The agency that helps a politician into high office is very well placed when it comes to pitching for government business.

There is only one juicier plum for the image doctor, but unfortunately there is nothing much he can do about it in the way of speculative presentations or exploratory lunches. All he can hope for is that one day, one wonderful day, the client will realize that something needs to be done and that he is the man to do it. And when the call comes, as it might quite easily do, we will be able to see the traces of burned rubber all the way from the agency to the Buckingham Palace car park.

The Dance of
the Leviathans

134

Short of a major war or an international recession of epic proportions, it seems that nothing can stop the forces of marketing from making the world *a more convenient place to shop*. The global village will have its global village supermarket, stocked with comfortingly familiar names, and one of the horrors of being abroad—having to adapt to the local toilet paper—will be completely eradicated. Our preferred paper (strong, absorbent, and three times softer than other leading brands) will be there on the shelf to welcome us, no matter where we roam.

Perhaps we have not quite reached that high point of civilization yet, but we will. There is an inevitability about the future that is plain to see after the progress that has been made during the past twenty years.

The giant clients will continue to root around in the marketing undergrowth of less-developed countries, setting up outposts and squashing or gobbling up small local competitors. And marching with them every step of the way will be the advertising conglomerates, taking over or merging with any agencies that have managed to remain independent, dousing them with money and shares until they can resist no longer.

Meanwhile, the international media organizations will carry on planting their satellites in space and their dishes on earth so that it will be technically possible to watch those patron saints of hygiene, the mad housewives from Cincinnati, comparing their stained garments anywhere in the world. For more literate consumers, the coverage of lifestyle magazines will expand, and *Architectural Digest* shall cover the earth.

Research companies will have the world's likes and dislikes (graded on a scale of one to ten) stored in their computers so that statistical-probability curves can be produced instantly for anything from weaning Eskimos off blubber and onto fish sticks to the sales potential of high-fiber breakfast cereals in China.

The staples of life—soluble aspirin, carbonated drinks, polyunsaturated spreads, and tasty deep-frozen TV dinners—will be available everywhere. It will be a dream come true, globalization in full flower.

It is not unreasonable to assume that within the next two decades the advertising business will no longer be made up of hundreds of agencies chasing thousands of clients. After consolidating and rationalizing, there may be as few as twenty agency groups, billion-dollar leviathans circling each other as they look for an opportunity to lumber in and steal one of the two hundred or so worthwhile global accounts. This situation will produce results that a few die-hard reactionaries might find offensive, but progress is never without its critics.

It is obvious that national characteristics will have to be modified if they don't happen to fit in with the grand design. For instance, the French housewife's ridiculously inefficient habit of buying fresh food every day from small shops will have to go. (In fact, it's already going. In 1989, for the first time, supermarkets accounted for just over 50 percent of food sales in France.) And that is only one of hundreds of awkward little local quirks that have made the global village such an untidy, fragmented market in the past. With determination and perseverance, most of them can be dealt with. It's just a matter of educating the consumer.

Unfortunately, there is one persistent inconvenience that may take a generation or more to get rid of, and that is the irritating problem of different languages. In an ideal marketing world, we would all speak globalese, and early examples of this media-efficient dialect can be seen gracing the walls of international airports and the pages of in-flight magazines. It is recognizable—barely, in some cases—as English, and it is based on the lowest common denominator principle of communication, the kind of message that a gifted six-year-old copywriter might dash off in between watching videos.

The Japanese, ingenious as ever, have been credited with pioneering the most distinctive style of mangled English, but other multinational marketeers and their agencies have been catching up fast. It is not, as you might think, arrived at by illiteracy or accident, and if we visit the headquarters of a giant client, we can see how globalese is created.

Allied Biscuits (now renamed Global Biscuits) has markets throughout the world, and the board has been advised by the agency to consider the advantages of basing its advertising on a single theme. The agency has produced statistics showing that consumers in general, and biscuit eaters in particular, are traveling more and more. Habitual biscuit eaters (the heavy users) are likely to eat biscuits on their travels. These are the opinion formers in the biscuit hierarchy, and if they can be converted into *brand-loyal* opinion formers, they will convert others.

How do we reach them? There is a great deal of discussion about the *cumulative international impact* of one consistent message. It is a promotionally sound theory and—here's one for the financial director—very cost-effective, since much of the basic material can be centrally produced and massive economies of scale (what a fabulous phrase) can be achieved. Also, a single worldwide campaign is just what we need to establish the product as an international biscuit, with all the inherent glamour and excitement associated with international products.

The board nods. It makes marketing sense. This is where the future of Global Biscuits lies. Rather than fritter away the world advertising budget on dozens of buckshot campaigns in dozens of languages sprinkled across dozens of countries, how much more . . . well, *impactful* . . . it will be to concentrate every resource behind one giant promotional thrust, a powerful single-language promise, irresistible to biscuit lovers everywhere.

Not all biscuit lovers, of course, are fluent in English. But 58 percent of Global Biscuits' sales are in North Amer-

137

ica and other English-speaking countries, and most Europeans have a smattering of English. The rest of the world will soon get the hang of it if they see it often enough. There is almost a case here for an extra few million to be added to the budget, for educational purposes.

English it shall be, then, although we can't afford to get too complicated. Brilliant simplicity is the thing, and so the agency is sent away to ruminate and give birth to something brilliantly simple.

The constraints on the creative department are considerable. Words of more than two syllables (with the exception of the magic word *international*) should be avoided. No puns or any wordplay of the kind that might puzzle a biscuit eater from Bologna or Dubai. No local references. No testimonials from local celebrities (the big Hollywood stars are acceptable, but it's doubtful if we could get Sylvester Stallone to nibble biscuits). Nothing that might upset vocal minority groups. Nothing with old people, unless they are very picturesque. Nothing that demands a sense of humor to be appreciated. Nothing too subtle.

Let's see now. Things Go Better with Global Biscuits? The Right Biscuit? The World's Favorite Biscuit? The Best Biscuit Money Can Buy? Top Leader Biscuit for the Modern Man? The Biscuit of the Future? The Biscuit Lover's Biscuit? The International Passport to Biscuit Pleasure?

Sadly, these jewels have already been claimed, which is a pity, since any of them could be used just as easily for biscuits as for soft drinks, liquor, airlines, or cigarettes. They all have that marvelously anodyne boastfulness that would have been perfect for all our purposes. Ah well.

The search continues for the universally acceptable,

universally comprehensible, universally persuasive phrase until something suitably harmless and all-embracing has been cobbled together, the millions can be unleashed, and globalese can take another step forward.

We might ask ourselves why the cream of the world's copywriting talent should be content to spend weeks or months laboring in a verbal kindergarten, but their willingness to do so is only part of the global agency's relationship with its global clients. Now that budgets are measured in tens of millions, the stakes are far too high to permit any more of that old-fashioned nonsense that happened in the cottage-industry days when agencies thought of themselves as equal working partners.

In the new mammoth agencies, there may be the outward appearance of power that comes from size, but in daily contact with their mammoth clients they must be careful not to forget their place. A certain suppleness is necessary, which, in anatomical terms, can be described as the posture of the bended knee.

This has always existed in advertising, and some packaged goods and automotive clients have been notorious for years because of their insistence on the master/slave relationship. With the arrogance of people in charge of large amounts of someone else's money, they have been known to reduce entire agencies to nervous wrecks. It used to be a malady confined to relatively few agencies and their famously autocratic clients, and it was regarded with horror and disbelief by the rest of the business. But in this tough new world where the loss of one global account means the loss of untold millions of income, we are likely to see the posture of the bended knee reaching epidemic levels.

Visible results of the deep knee bend invariably show up in the advertising. Look behind any vainglorious and clumsy campaign and you will usually find a dictator in charge of the budget. (Very occasionally this can produce brilliant advertising, but brilliant dictators were always rare, and globalization will probably make them extinct.) A more polished but equally dreary piece of advertising—the marketing strategy set to music—is normally the product of committee work, and committees can be every bit as daft and bullying as dictators.

Why do clients like this bother with agencies? Why keep the dog if you intend to do all the yapping yourself? Because it's less expensive. You don't have to pay for those acres of office space, and you can fire agencies without any problems of redundancy compensation. And, as a recreational bonus, you can kick agencies around with complete impunity. They won't kick back, and they're never likely to be in a position to affect your career.

If this unpleasant development in client/agency relationships should become increasingly widespread, and there is no obvious reason why it shouldn't, we will see some changes not just in the standards of advertising around the world but in the type of person who wants to work in the business.

Historically, advertising has attracted individualists, entrepreneurs, and talented misfits. They came to advertising partly because it offered larger and faster rewards than other occupations, but mainly because it was more fun than other occupations, and they felt at home in it. Informal, unpredictable, and dependent on individual skills and creativity, it matched their personalities. It was an interesting and lucrative way of living by your wits.

But as the business becomes more structured, more respectable, more governed by money and corporate jockeying than by ideas, so it will lose its appeal for the individualist. A different animal will inhabit agency offices: The new advertising man, brought up on globalization and the need to maintain dividends and share prices, will take over. He will be good at meetings, adroit at politics, prudent, measured, solid, reliable—a carbon copy of his counterpart at Global Biscuits. And when that happens, working in advertising will be exactly like working in any other international business peddling an international commodity.

A ghastly prospect indeed, and it is enough to make the mythical young man with a bright idea think twice about trying to persuade a susceptible industrialist to give him a chance. And yet, human nature being relentlessly optimistic, it's just possible that we haven't quite reached the stage when advertising can be thrown into the same gray pit as insurance or the civil service. Perhaps all is not lost. . . .

Somewhere in Tribeca, three young men are having lunch. Bored and frustrated with their jobs in mammoth agencies, they are planning to break away and start their own tiny but highly creative enterprise. Creativity has been in hibernation for so long that it could be awakened and sold as something new, something a brand manager has never seen in his working life.

There is reason to believe that one or two minor pieces of business, just enough to keep the new enterprise afloat, could be persuaded by a good-enough pitch to leave the mammoth and join the minnow. A friendly bank manager has been lined up. The future looks rosy. Another bottle of wine is ordered.

There is only one slight problem. Should the new

agency be called Me, You & Him? You, Him & Me? Him, Me & You? It's nothing to fall out over (not yet, anyway), but we all know what happens to the last name on the list.